THE CHILDREN OF LOOKED AFTER CHILDREN

Outcomes, Experiences and Ensuring Meaningful Support to Young Parents In and Leaving Care

Louise Roberts

First published in Great Britain in 2021 by

Policy Press, an imprint of
Bristol University Press
University of Bristol
1–9 Old Park Hill
Bristol
BS2 8BB
UK
t: +44 (0)117 954 5940
e: bup-info@bristol.ac.uk

Details of international sales and distribution partners are available at
policy.bristoluniversitypress.co.uk

© Bristol University Press 2021

The digital PDF and ePub versions of this title are available Open Access and distributed under the terms of the Creative Commons Attribution- NonCommercial 4.0 licence (http://creativecommons. org/licenses/by- nc/4.0/) which permits adaptation, alteration, reproduction and distribution for non-commercial use, without further permission provided the original work is attributed. The derivative works do not need to be licenced on the same terms.

British Library Cataloguing in Publication Data
A catalogue record for this book is available from the British Library

ISBN 978-1-4473-5429-1 hardcover
ISBN 978-1-4473-5432-1 OA ePub
ISBN 978-1-4473-5430-7 OA PDF

The right of Louise Roberts to be identified as author of this work has been asserted by her in accordance with the Copyright, Designs and Patents Act 1988.

All rights reserved: no part of this publication may be reproduced, stored in a retrieval system, or transmitted in any form or by any means, electronic, mechanical, photocopying, recording, or otherwise without the prior permission of Bristol University Press.

Every reasonable effort has been made to obtain permission to reproduce copyrighted material. If, however, anyone knows of an oversight, please contact the publisher.

The statements and opinions contained within this publication are solely those of the author and not of the University of Bristol or Bristol University Press. The University of Bristol and Bristol University Press disclaim responsibility for any injury to persons or property resulting from any material published in this publication.

Bristol University Press and Policy Press work to counter discrimination on grounds of gender, race, disability, age and sexuality.

Cover design: Liam Roberts
Front cover image: Shutterstock_385484236
Bristol University Press and Policy Press use environmentally responsible print partners.
Printed and bound in Great Britain by CPI Group (UK) Ltd, Croydon, CR0 4YY

For L and F

Contents

List of tables		vi
About the author and contributors		vii
Acknowledgements		viii
1	Introduction	1
2	Early pregnancy risk and missed opportunities to plan for parenthood	15
3	Outcomes for parents in and leaving care: parenting 'success' and corporate parenting failure	41
4	Professional perspectives: assessing parenting potential and managing dual responsibilities	55
5	The experiences of parents: hopes, anxieties and reflections	73
6	Responding to diverse needs: support availability, sustainability and acceptability	95
7	Conclusion: if this were my child	123
References		143
Index		159

List of tables

2.1	Prevalence of sexual health behaviours by living arrangement 2015	20
2.2	Odds ratios for the association between foster care and sexual health behaviours	23
2.3	Prevalence of sexual health behaviours by living arrangement 2017	26
2.4	Odds ratios for the association between being in care and sexual health behaviours	29
3.1	Descriptive statistics for study variables by care leaver status of birth parents	45
3.2	Relationship status of parents	48
3.3	The number and nature of recorded needs for young people	48
3.4	Living arrangements of children	49
6.1	The number and nature of recorded needs for young people	98

About the author and contributors

The author

Louise Roberts is Lecturer in Social Work at Cardiff University. She is part of the CASCADE Leadership Network and her research interests are broadly connected to social work with children and families. As a registered social worker, Louise is particularly interested in the relationship between the state and the family. This includes policies and practices designed to prevent children from entering the care system, as well as the role of the state as parent.

Contributors to Chapter 2

Rebecca Anthony is Research Associate based within the Centre for the Development and Evaluation of Complex Intervention for Public Health Improvement (DECIPHer) at Cardiff University. Her research interests are in the area of improving outcomes for children, with a focus on children and young people 'looked after' and adopted.

Sara Jayne Long is Research Associate based within the Centre for the Development and Evaluation of Complex Intervention for Public Health Improvement (DECIPHer) at Cardiff University. She is an interdisciplinary researcher interested in health, wellbeing and education outcomes of children and young people.

Honor Young is Lecturer in quantitative research methods at Cardiff University. She is based within the Centre for the Development and Evaluation of Complex Intervention for Public Health Improvement (DECIPHer). Her research interests include young people's sexual health, sexual risk-taking behaviour, and dating and relationship violence.

Acknowledgements

This book would not have been possible without the support of many people. First, to everyone who participated in the research: thank you to the professionals who supported the project, who granted me access and who gave their time to talk about their experiences; special thanks to the parents who welcomed me into their homes and were willing to share highly personal and sometimes painful experiences with me. I will always be grateful and hope you all find peace and happiness in the future.

I am especially grateful to everyone at Voices from Care Cymru, for giving me the initial idea for the research, and for providing regular guidance and consultation along the way. Particular thanks to Chris Dunn and Fran Minty, and to Deborah Jones, for being so passionate and eager to use the findings to campaign for change.

The work has benefited from regular consultation with young people and parents. Thank you to the members of the Parents Advisory Group, facilitated by Voices from Care Cymru, who have supported the project for its duration. Special thanks to Jen, who has been with me throughout this journey, offered invaluable insights, and whose commitment to campaigning for change has been inspirational. Thank you also to members of the Alpha Group, CASCADE Voices, as well as members of parents advisory groups at Family Rights Group and the National Youth Advocacy Service (NYAS) Cymru.

Thank you to the people who supported applications and read drafts, helped develop my arguments and questioned my thinking. This includes Health and Care Research Wales, my colleagues and friends at CASCADE and Cardiff University. Particular thanks to Donald Forrester, Dawn Mannay, Alyson Rees, Jonathan Scourfield and Rachael Vaughan, as well as Elaine Chase, Caroline Cresswell, Carol Floris, Sally Holland, Louise Howe, Sally Jenkins, Lynette Jones, Sharon Lovell, Zoe Morgan, Lisa Morriss, Jackie Murphy, June Statham, Rachel Thomas and Lucy Treby.

Thank you also to the people I have previously collaborated with in the development of journal articles connected to this issue: Martin Elliott, Donald Forrester, Sara Jayne Long, Nina Maxwell, Sarah Meekings, Graham Moore, Gillian Hewitt, Simon Murphy, Kathryn Shelton, Audra Smith and Honor Young. Your work and contribution to this book is recognised.

Finally, to my family: thanks for believing in me and being there for me, this project has reminded me how important that is.

1

Introduction

For all parents, regardless of age or care experience, the onset of parenthood can be a time of hope and excitement, but it can also induce anxieties, present challenges and prompt changes. Practical issues associated with having a baby need to be considered, such as the impact on work or education routines, finances, living arrangements, as well as acquiring the necessary baby-related equipment, furniture and clothing and adhering to the comprehensive schedules of antenatal health appointments and checks. In addition to pragmatic considerations, individuals or couples may need to emotionally adapt to the prospect of parenthood, mentally adjusting to changes in relationships, identity, responsibility and priorities. For many, this exciting yet simultaneously terrifying journey will be made easier with the support and reassurance of family and friends.

The idea for this research study came from young people and adults involved with Voices from Care Cymru (VfCC), 'a national, independent, Welsh organisation, dedicated to upholding the rights and welfare of care experienced children and young people' (vfcc.org.uk). Over time, individuals connected to VfCC had become concerned about the experiences and support available to young people in and leaving care when they became parents. For many of these young people, the discovery of pregnancy was a happy event and, despite some initial trepidation, they looked forward to starting families of their own. Yet in addition to the practical, emotional and health-related considerations already noted, the organisation was concerned that care-experienced parents-to-be shared some additional difficulties and experiences. These included the potential for social work intervention, experiences of stigma and discrimination, as well as reduced access to resources and support. While the organisation was keen to acknowledge and champion the successes of parents who overcame multiple adversities and maintained the care of their children, they were nevertheless deeply concerned about the numbers subject to routine assessment, monitoring and intervention, including permanent and compulsory separation.

In highlighting this issue as an area for research, VfCC were keen to know more about pregnancy and parenthood for parents in and leaving care. This included broader understandings of the experiences of parents and their reflections on who or what helped, what hindered, and where, as well as what, support was available. In addition, the organisation was keen that the research confirm or deny their suspicion that care-experienced parents were disproportionately more likely to experience social work intervention and/or separation from their children.

My interest in and commitment to the research

The extent to which researchers in social science can and should be objective is subject to debate. For qualitative researchers it has been argued that it is neither possible nor desirable to protect research from the influence of personal values (Lichtman 2010). In the interests of transparency, I intend to make explicit my interest and motivation to undertake this study at the outset.

First, the origins of the research are important to me, reflecting both my personal aspirations as a researcher, as well as those of the centre in which I am based within Cardiff University. The Children's Social Care Research and Development Centre (CASCADE) aims 'to bridge divides between academic research, government policy and practitioner and service user need, to maximise the impact and influence of research evidence, and to enable wide audiences to access the results of research' (Staples et al 2019: 197). Likewise, the development of CASCADE Voices (a research advisory group made up of care-experienced young people) sought to embed the views and perspectives of care-experienced young people within the centre's work and beyond (see Staples et al 2019). In this way, the identification of the research topic by 'experts by experience' (Preston-Shoot 2007), the potential for young people to adopt consultative as well as participative roles in the project (further details in the following sections) as well as the potential to positively influence policy and practice, had considerable appeal to me as a researcher.

Second, I have some personal interest and connection to this issue. As argued by Dwyer and Buckle (2009: 54):

> The issue of researcher membership in the group or area being studied is relevant to all approaches of qualitative methodology as the researcher plays such a direct and intimate role in both data collection and analysis. Whether the researcher is an insider, sharing the characteristic, role, or experience under study with the participants, or an outsider to the commonality shared by participants, the personhood

of the researcher, including her or his membership status in relation to those participating in the research, is an essential and ever-present aspect of the investigation.

Following the example of Palmer (2019), I have sought to reflect on my membership status and consider areas of similarity and difference between myself and the participants.

I do not have experience of the care system. I have a relatively small but close family and growing up there was no real shortage of love, support or money. In school I was academically able and I have clear memories of being told that I would go to university and could achieve whatever I wanted in life. The optimism attached to my potential future prospects was severely challenged when, at 16, I found out I was pregnant. Without going into the specific circumstances and details, it is fair to say that this experience was one that caused significant strain for my family. There were differing and changing measures of anger, shame, sadness, disappointment and anxiety. If I am honest, while I understood these emotions towards me, I could not understand the unhappiness at the impending arrival of a baby. For me, a baby was a reason to be joyful and, despite the animosity, I looked forward to being a mother. I felt very protective of my child, I imagined all the things we would do and the type of parent I would be. I felt proud that I had chosen to take on this challenge and believed that my goals and aspirations did not need to be compromised.

Looking back now, I smile at my determined and resolute attitude. As someone who thinks in multiple shades of grey, and rarely sees things in black and white, I have never been more confident in a decision. I have no doubt that I made the right choice for me, but there is also no doubt that I was naïve. I was unprepared for how hard being a parent was, how relentless it would be, how exhausted I would feel and how envious I would be of the continuing freedoms of my friends. I was also conscious of the pervasive stigma connected to being a young parent, and concerned that judgements were not only directed at me, but also at my child.

Luckily for me, and despite initial reactions, I had lots of support. My family helped me attend health appointments, supported me through labour and helped me to purchase the long list of baby-related equipment. I had no housing concerns as it was assumed I would remain with my parents and I was protected from managing any household bills or chores. I was supported to return to school, supported to drive and given access to a car that enabled me to travel easily and quickly between the childminder and school, and later university. I had people to call on if I was having a bad day (or night), who would tell me to go and have a cup of tea when I felt I couldn't cope. I had people to turn to if I had a question about colic, sleep routines, feeding, bathing, nappy rash, tantrums ... My family also allowed me space to be a teenager and I had a weekly night out with my friends. I had a partner who loved us both and was in it with me.

In addition to the support of family and friends, I was entitled to welfare benefits. I was able to claim a maternity grant, income support, child benefit and received free milk tokens. The option of local social housing was available, although not needed. University education was free and I was entitled to a means-tested grant to support my studies. If I were in the same situation today, state support would not be so generous, or so easy to access.

This relatively detailed account of my personal experience may be a somewhat unusual opener for a social science book of this nature. Yet such reflections foreground important considerations, including individual hopes and struggles, with respect to parenthood, the relevance of social, economic and cultural capital (Bourdieu 1984), as well as normative values and judgements with respect to parenthood. They also demonstrate some insider status based on lived experience of mothering 'on the margins' and the pursuit of 'respectable motherhood' (Mannay 2014; Mannay et al 2018).

Yet the simplistic nature of insider/outsider distinctions is acknowledged. As noted by Wolf (1996: 16) there is potential for researchers to feel 'neither insider or outsider or both simultaneously.' Similarly, Dwyer and Buckle's (2009) notion of 'the space between' also has resonance. Reflecting on potential differences in experience between myself and the parent participants, there is recognition that the practical, emotional and financial resources that were available to me, are frequently unavailable, unstable or changeable for parents in and leaving care. Likewise, I have not experienced the label of 'looked after' or 'care-experienced' (Mannay et al 2017; Burns 2018), nor do I have personal experience of corporate parenting. I have not endured sexual, physical, emotional abuse and/or neglect. My upbringing and childhood experiences have not been a source of doubt regarding my ability to parent. I have not been assessed in a mother and baby unit, experienced trauma, domestic violence, drug and alcohol use and/or mental health difficulties. I have not been subject to professional scrutiny and assessment and have not faced the strains of poverty and poor housing. Further adding to the complexity, the passage of time has changed my experience of parenting. The vast majority of pressures and anxieties I once experienced, have diminished. My progression through higher education, my training as a social worker and current employment as a lecturer has afforded me professional status and freed me of concerns regarding respectability and marginalisation (Mannay 2014; Mannay et al 2018). In this way, any claim to insider knowledge of this area is recognised as both limited and temporal.

Overview of the study

This book is based on a research study which took place within CASCADE at Cardiff University, between October 2014 and March 2019. Funded by Health and Care Research Wales, the study was divided into several stages and incorporated a mixed method design. The study was specifically concerned with the Welsh context and each of the 22 local authorities in Wales participated in one or more phases. Ethical approval was granted by Cardiff University's Social Research Ethics Committee.

The study sought to prioritise the views and perspectives of 'experts by experience' (Preston-Shoot 2007). This included involving care-experienced young people in both advisory and participatory roles within the study. For its duration, the study was supported by an advisory group of care-experienced parents. The study sought to provide detailed accounts of parents' views and perspectives as presented by these participants. As argued by Rubin and Rubin (2012: 3), in-depth qualitative interviewing allows researchers to 'explore in detail the experiences, motives and opinions of others and learn to see the world from perspectives other than their own'. Related to this, the study also sought to include the reflections of social care professionals; professionals with experience of working with parents in and leaving care, and with knowledge of corporate parenting responsibilities and capabilities.

As argued by Cresswell and Plano Clark (2011), mixed methods designs are advantageous in producing more evidence and answering more questions than qualitative or quantitative designs alone. Through the collection of survey data and secondary analysis of national data sets, the study sought to investigate the issue at a national as well as individual scale. In this way, it was hoped that the design would speak to multiple audiences and answer multiple questions with respect to outcomes, experience and support.

The research study incorporated the following phases: stage one provided an introduction into some of the key issues and concerns of parents in and leaving care. Eight exploratory interviews were conducted with care-experienced parents. Although not part of the initial grant proposal, at the outset of the study, some parents had requested opportunity to participate in the research and to speak about their experiences. The initial interviews provided a valuable foundation from which to approach the remainder of the study. Two third-sector agencies, with a support remit spanning south and west Wales, facilitated parents' participation in a qualitative interview. Two parents were the primary carers for their children but six had experienced the permanent and compulsory removal of their child/ren. At the time of interview, 12 of the 16 children born to the participants were also in care or had been adopted.

Stage two was concerned with existing evidence and involved a review of the international literature. The review included literature from published and unpublished sources with a focus on parent and professional perspectives, risk and protective factors with respect to early pregnancy and parenthood and evidence regarding outcomes. It was hoped that this phase of the research would identify evaluations of supportive interventions designed for parents in and leaving care. Yet, despite repeated 'calls to action' (Fallon and Broadhurst, 2015: 4) the evidence base with respect to 'what works' is underdeveloped.

Stage three was concerned with outcomes. First, qualitative interviews were undertaken with representatives of leaving-care services from each of the 22 local authorities across Wales. The interviews were designed to explore practice experience, as well as local support provision for young parents in and leaving care. In addition, 20 out of the 22 local authorities were asked to complete a survey for each young person who was pregnant or a parent, and who was currently eligible for support from the local authority as a child 'looked after' or leaving care. The survey required non-identifiable information but asked for details about parents' identified needs and support resources, as well as information about the living arrangements of children. This included questions as to whether children were in the care of their parents (with or without statutory involvement), or whether they were separated and the children were living with other family, local authority carers or had been adopted. This phase was designed to provide a 'snapshot' of the practice context in Wales, including current numbers of young parents, professional perceptions of risk and protective factors with respect to parenting, as well as the extent of additional support and intervention by statutory social services.

During this phase of the research, links were made with researchers working on the School Health Research Network health and wellbeing survey (see Long et al 2017) and the Wales Adoption Study (see Anthony et al, 2016). The School Health Research Network survey is a bi-annual survey of young people in secondary school in Wales concerned with health and wellbeing. Analysis of survey data from 2015 and 2017 was designed to examine sexual health outcomes and assess risk of early pregnancy for young people in care. The Wales Adoption Study comprised the records of all children placed for adoption by every local authority in Wales between 1 July 2014 and 31 July 2015 (n = 374). These records allowed an exploration of the numbers and needs of birth parents identified as care leavers.

Stage four was primarily concerned with the experiences of expectant and new parents. Thirty qualitative interviews were conducted with parents who were expecting a child or had a child under the age of one. Eight parents participated in a follow-up interview after a year and were able to reflect on how their situation had developed. In six instances, permission was given for interviews to be conducted with key supporting professionals. This stage was intended to generate rich data about young people's feelings and concerns, as well as their reflections on the experience of professional involvement and the availability of support.

The final stage of the study was concerned with generating recommendations for policy and practice. Over the course of the research, an advisory group of care-experienced parents has supported the project and provided valuable insight and advice regarding the potential for positive change. In addition, the study has sought input from a range of other individuals, including young people and parents, statutory and third-sector professionals. The research on which the book is based will be referred to as the Voices study in subsequent chapters.

Aims of the book

Several academic journal articles have been published over the course of the research (Roberts 2017, 2019; Roberts et al 2017, 2018, 2019). In the hope of making the research findings accessible to as wide an audience as possible, some of this material is presented again, along with new and unseen data. Importantly, this book is intended to bring the findings of each of the phases together and provide a holistic examination of pregnancy and parenthood for young people in and leaving care, with consideration of salient issues before, during and after young people become parents.

The book has three key aims. The first is to shine a light on pregnancy and parenthood for young people in and leaving care, and illuminate the need for policy and practice attention. The findings offer a valuable contribution to an underdeveloped evidence base, providing evidence of disadvantage, discrimination and poor outcomes. It is hoped that the national scope of the study, and its inclusion of mixed methods and multiple sources, provides robust and comprehensive consideration of the issue which is difficult for those in power to ignore. Furthermore, such focus has direct relevance to ongoing concerns with respect to child welfare inequalities (see Featherstone et al 2017; Morris et al 2018; Bywaters et al 2020; Elliott 2020), accusations that the state is both punitive and neglectful (Featherstone et al 2018), together with long-standing and persistent increases in the numbers of children 'looked after' and a system described to be 'in crisis' and 'out of control' (Bilson et al 2017; *Care Crisis Review* 2018; Thomas 2018).

Second, the book is intended to provide a platform for the voices of care-experienced parents. Whether parents have encountered relatively few or significant difficulties as parents, their voices provide poignant insight into the lived experience of pregnancy and parenting. Parents' reflections include heart-breaking accounts of loss and grief, as well heart-warming stories of love and overcoming hardship. While concerns about disadvantage, outcomes and support quite rightly sit at the core of this book, so too is a wish to recognise and celebrate the examples where parents 'successfully' care for their children, despite adversity and without statutory involvement. Crucially, parents' perspectives should form the foundation from which to consider developments to policy and practice.

Finally, the book seeks to be a useful resource for professionals and policy makers. From the outset of the study there has been widespread recognition of the importance of this issue from professionals across both the statutory and third sectors. The book is not intended to be unhelpfully critical of practice, or demonise individual practitioners or agencies. The inclusion of statutory professionals in the development and conduct of this study has enabled some of the challenges and dilemmas facing practitioners to be elucidated. As described by Pithouse (1987), social work is largely an 'invisible trade'. Making explicit the obligations, competing tensions, anxieties and constraints faced by professionals, provides a valuable opportunity to reflect, debate and hopefully improve.

Recurring themes and questions

The book prompts consideration of parenting 'success' for young people in and leaving care. Outcomes provide an important way of assessing 'success' for parents and these are analysed both in terms of pregnancy planning as well as the living arrangements and legal status of children born to parents in and leaving care. However, a more critical consideration of 'success' is also encouraged, with readers urged to think about what 'success' could and should entail. For example, in addition to considerations of whether parents are separated or retain care of their children, definitions of 'success' may also be influenced by individual wellbeing and the quality of parent–child relationship. Levels of poverty, standards and security of housing, the availability of emotional and informal support, and the nature and degree of professional involvement are also arguably key considerations. In this way, a holistic consideration of parenting 'success' is offered, taking into account outcomes, as well as the nature of parents' experiences and lived realities.

Related to considerations of 'success', the book also focuses on the role, responsibilities and responses of the state. Helpful in this vein is Lorraine Fox Harding's (1997) classic typology of value perspectives considering the relationship between the state and the family. While it was recognised that administrations tend not to adopt one of the following perspectives exclusively, the typology is nevertheless useful in conceptualising the nature and purpose of state intervention and involvement:

- Laissez faire and patriarchy – state involvement in family life is minimal and parents are afforded maximum rights.
- State paternalism and child protection – state involvement in family life minimises parents' rights and is legitimate in order to protect children.
- Defence of the birth family and parents' rights – state intervention recognises parents' rights and seeks to support families.
- Children's rights – state recognises the child is an independent person with individual rights.

In this book, Fox Harding's categorisation will aid understanding of the relationship between the state and care-experienced parents. Readers are encouraged to consider the reflections of parents and professionals, and to assess whether they suggest minimal state involvement or interest, whether they can be interpreted as efforts to support parents or protect children, and whether support responses are designed to prioritise the needs and rights of the child.

While Fox Harding's (1997) model provides a way of considering the state–family relationship, the book also argues that the relationship between the state and the family is somewhat different for parents in and leaving care. In theory, the state's effort to both support families and protect children are applicable to any or all parents, regardless of history or background. More recently, Forrester (2020) has argued the need for minimal intervention in family life. Yet the applicability of this is more problematic for parents in and leaving care, as the state is also their parent and primary source of support.

Bullock et al (2006) have previously argued that the notion of corporate parenting should be considered 'an impersonal entity' and tasks in relation to parenting shared across a number of individuals and delivered at national, local and personal levels. Responsibilities of the state as parent extend to all public bodies and corporate parenting responsibilities are not and should not be thought of as the responsibility of Children's Services in isolation. Bullock et al's (2006) proposition is helpful in providing a framework for encouraging consideration of the multiple organisations and individuals with corporate parenting responsibilities.

Over the course of the book, the extent to which such responsibilities are recognised and the array of resources and connections utilised, will be considered. In this way, the book explores whether the responses and resources available from corporate parents serve to help or hinder notions of parenting 'success'. Related to this, readers are prompted to question whether the state's parenting is 'good enough' and if the responses and support available to parents would be considered 'good enough for my child' (Welsh Government 2018: 79). Readers are encouraged to continually consider if the support responses or expectations placed upon parents in and leaving care differ from those of other young parents supported by their families. This includes examining the potential for parents to be stigmatised because of their care status and discriminated against because of their care histories.

A note on language

Language is important. As noted by Wakeman (2019: 71): 'Language has always played an important role in the generation of stigma, as well as in combatting it. Language can be used intentionally or unintentionally to communicate a message about a person or group of people as being "other" and to perpetuate stigma.' Such comments are pertinent for this book. For example, it has previously been noted that young people in care can object to the acronym 'LAC' (looked after child) on the basis they are not 'LACking in anything' (Children's Commissioner for Wales, 2016). Similarly, terms such as 'looked after child' and 'care leaver' prioritise and accentuate young people's care status while, for children and young people, being in care constitutes only one part of their identity (Mannay et al 2015).

When considering language for this book, several terms were considered and each proved problematic. For example, 'care leaver parents' was appealing because it coincided with secondary analysis conducted on the Wales Adoption Study (see Roberts et al 2017 and Chapter 3), where birth parents were distinguished as 'care leaver parents' and 'non-care leaver parents' (based on whether they had been categorised as a care leaver in the Child Assessment Report for Adoption (CARA). While this term proved appropriate in this instance, it was unsuitable for wider use in the book because of the primary emphasis on 'care status' and because some young people become parents while in care, as opposed to while they are transitioning out of care.

The term 'young parents' was advantageous in avoiding accentuating care status. Yet it is recognised that this term is not neutral and can also be imbued with negative connotations (Action for Children 2017). Similarly, the focus of this research is specifically concerned with care experience and the extent to which this influences parents' needs, experiences and outcomes. In recent years, references to 'care experience' have gained popularity. The term is more inclusive for individuals who have current as well as historical experiences of care, and provides a subtle challenge to the defining nature of previous labels, through its emphasis of experience rather identity. Yet for the specific focus of the research, the term does not provide sufficient indication of the age of the parent or the ongoing responsibilities of the state with regard to corporate parenting. As this research is particularly concerned with young people who become parents when in or leaving care (under the age of 25) and while under the care of the local authority, 'care-experienced parents' was unsuitable as the principal term.

For these reasons, parents will predominantly be referred to as 'parents in and leaving care'. While not ideal in terms of brevity, the term positions young people as parents primarily, while also recognising their current care experience and status. However, in recognition of the tensions described, and in the interests of readability, references to care leaver parents and care-experienced parents will also be included where appropriate, as will references to young people simply as parents.

Structure and overview

The structure of the book is aligned with its key aims and the contents can be divided into three thematic sections. The first section (Chapters 2 and 3) is concerned with outcomes and aims to demonstrate why parenthood for young people in and leaving care is an issue requiring urgent policy and practice attention. The second section (Chapters 4 and 5) of the book focuses on experiences of pregnancy and parenthood for young people in and leaving care, as well as those of professionals tasked with supporting them. This section brings to life challenges and rewards with respect to parenting for young people, as well as professional dilemmas and tensions. The final section (Chapters 6 and 7) is concerned with issues of support and considers future efforts to improve support responses for young people in and leaving care who are pregnant and parenting.

In the first section Chapter 2 considers early pregnancy for young people in and leaving care. It argues that, despite reductions in teenage pregnancy more widely, young people in and leaving care continue to be at increased risk. The chapter presents evidence from national surveys of young people which evidence that those in care experience poorer sexual health outcomes in comparison to their peers. The chapter also presents interview data from social care professionals, which suggests that in the current context such risks are unlikely to diminish. Challenges with respect to funding cuts and austerity are reported, together with practice tensions related to when and in what circumstances young people should be provided with sexual health advice and support. Professional perceptions of the potential to influence the trajectories of young people with regard to pregnancy and parenthood are also examined.

Chapter 3 considers outcomes for parents in and leaving care. Findings from the Wales Adoption Study are presented. The analysis identifies the numbers of birth parents who were recorded as care leavers and argues that they are over-represented among birth parents whose children were placed for adoption. In addition, the chapter presents survey data collected from leaving-care teams across Wales. Designed to provide a 'snapshot' of care-experienced parents, the findings highlight the potential for multiple and multifaceted support needs. While the majority of young people in and leaving care were caring for their children, independently or with Children's Services involvement, an alarming number of parents were separated from their children, who were living with family members, local authority carers or adoptive parents.

In the second section Chapter 4 presents data from professionals with experience of supporting parents in and leaving care. The chapter examines the assessment and planning considerations that are enacted at the onset of pregnancy. The potential for stigma and discrimination will be revisited, together with professionals' perceptions of barriers to and facilitators of 'successful' parenting. The chapter also explores competing tensions experienced by professionals in seeking to support young people as well as adhere to safeguarding responsibilities. While professionals recognised the importance of ensuring the safety and wellbeing of children, many also highlighted the potential for a more proactive and supportive corporate parent and grandparent.

Chapter 5 focuses on the experiences of care-experienced parents. It offers detailed accounts of young people's reactions on finding out they were going to be parents, their hopes and anxieties in this regard, and reflections on practical as well as emotional needs. The chapter also details young people's perceptions of stigma and discrimination as well as the availability of support and advice. The chapter engages with the perspectives of parents, who, despite periods of significant anxiety and adversity, were successfully caring for their children. In addition, the chapter also considers the experiences of those separated from their children, who had limited input and influence in their children's lives.

In the third section, Chapter 6 is concerned with support. Little is known about what support is wanted by parents in and leaving care, nor what is effective in promoting parenting 'success'. This chapter presents data collected over the course of the research study, highlighting both variable support needs as well as variable support services. The chapter also explores challenges in relation to support development. This includes providing support which is responsive to the diverse needs of parents and children, and which is wanted by parents and is non-stigmatising. In addition, the difficulty of securing financial commitment for such developments in a context of ever scarce resources, as well as uneven and unstable numbers of pregnant and parenting young people, is acknowledged. Despite this, the chapter offers examples of best practice through case examples from parents and professionals about the opportunities for both small and significant changes to better support and promote parenting success for young people in and leaving care.

Chapter 7 revisits key findings from the book. It argues that the state as corporate parent has too long been blind to young people's increased risk of pregnancy and too accepting of their increased hardship and disadvantage. The chapter argues that evidence with respect to continued risk of early pregnancy and poor outcomes as parents warrants immediate policy and practice attention. The chapter contends that many of the issues raised by professionals and parents over the course of the research will resonate with all parents, regardless of age or care experience. Yet the resources parents in and leaving care have available, and their experiences of stigma, do not typically mirror those of other parents, and put them at distinct disadvantage in terms of parenting 'success'.

The chapter ends with a series of recommendations for policy and practice development. These recommendations have been co-produced with care-experienced and non-care-experienced young people and parents as well as professionals in both the statutory and third sectors. It is hoped that these suggestions will kickstart meaningful improvements at individual, organisational and national levels. The book concludes with a section written by a care-experienced parent, who has been part of the advisory group for the duration of the research. The section offers a final personalised plea for ongoing policy and practice development.

2

Early pregnancy risk and missed opportunities to plan for parenthood

Co-authored with Rebecca Anthony, Sara Jayne Long and Honor Young

Introduction and background

This chapter considers sexual health outcomes and risk of early pregnancy for young people in and leaving care. At the outset of the Voices study, the intention was to focus only on early parenthood for care-experienced young people. Yet in order to fully consider these issues in relation to parenting, it is important to understand the context in which young people become parents. This includes considering both if and why young people in and leaving care face increased risk of early pregnancy and parenthood.

Research evidence has long shown young people who have lived in foster care, residential care and kinship care to be more likely to become young parents than those who have not (Svoboda 2012). Although research studies vary in terms of scope and size, Fallon and Broadhurst's (2015: 11) evidence review concluded that 'the weight of available international evidence suggests that children in or in the process of leaving care are at elevated risk of teenage pregnancy and early transition to parenthood'. Examples of such evidence include studies from Australia (Cashmore and Paxman 1996, 2007; Lima et al 2019), Canada (Turpel-Lafond and Kendall 2009), Spain (Del Valle et al 2008; Roca et al 2009), Sweden (Vinnerljung and Sallnäs 2008), the United States (US) (Oshima et al 2013; King et al 2014) as well as a comparative study of Germany, Finland and Great Britain (Cameron et al 2018).

Evidence from the US also includes the Midwest Study, a study which sought to track the progress of over 700 young people leaving care across three North American states, Illinois, Iowa and Wisconsin (Courtney et al 2011). The findings illustrated significantly higher rates of pregnancy and parenthood for young people leaving care, in comparison with the general population. By age 19, nearly half of the females leaving care reported experiencing pregnancy, compared to 20 per cent of the general population (Courtney et al 2005), and by age 21, this had increased to 71 per cent compared to 33 per cent (Courtney et al 2007). At ages 19 and 21, young people leaving care were approximately twice as likely as their peers to report having at least one living child (Courtney et al 2005, 2007). A review of 56 US studies concluded that young people with foster care experience, as well as being more likely to experience early pregnancy and parenthood, were also at increased risk of engaging in risky sexual behaviour, earlier experience of sexual activity, sexually transmitted infections, transactional sex and repeat pregnancy in the short term (Winter et al 2016).

Evidence from the United Kingdom (UK) is consistent with international findings. Biehal and Wade's (1992) study in England, involved 183 young people leaving care aged between 16 and 18. Almost a quarter (23 per cent) of the young women were parents at the point of leaving care and this proportion increased to almost 50 per cent when a sub-sample were followed up within 24 months (Biehal and Wade 1996). Similarly, Dixon et al's (2006) study of 106 young people leaving care from across seven local authorities in England showed that within 13 months of leaving care 35 per cent of females were pregnant or parenting, and 15 per cent of males were expectant or current fathers.

Highlighting the increased risk of early pregnancy for young people in and leaving care, an audit of teenage pregnancies in Wales over a one-year period, found that the proportion of conceptions for young people in care was over five times that for young people not in care. The authors also found that care-experienced young people were more likely than their peers to continue, rather than terminate, the pregnancy (Craine et al 2014). Comparable findings have been noted by Dworsky and deCoursey (2009), whose analysis of US administrative data suggested that approximately 90 per cent of pregnancies for care-experienced young people proceed to birth.

Efforts to reduce teenage pregnancy

While there has been an accumulation of evidence showing young people in and leaving care to be at risk of early pregnancy and parenthood, it is also important to consider the sustained policy efforts in England and Wales which have sought to reduce rates of teenage pregnancy (Social Exclusion Unit 1999; Department for

Education and Skills and Department of Health 2006; Department for Children, Schools and Families and Department of Health 2010; Welsh Government 2010; Welsh Government 2012; Department for Education 2015; Public Health Wales 2016). This policy emphasis is aimed at all young people (not specifically those with care experience) and seeks to avoid the range of social, economic, education and health inequalities associated with teenage pregnancy (Swann et al 2003).

Policy commitments to reduce early pregnancy rates have shown evidence of success; conception rates in England and Wales are currently at their lowest level since 1969 with sizeable and consistent reductions for both under-16s (conception rates reduced by 67 per cent between 2007 and 2017) and under-18s (conception rates reduced by 57 per cent between 2007 and 2017) (Office for National Statistics 2019). It is nevertheless important to note that pregnancy rates in the UK continue to compare unfavourably with those in Western Europe (Office for National Statistics 2017). It is also unclear how effective such policies have been specifically for young people in and leaving care.

As noted by Cook and Cameron (2015: 243) teenage pregnancy can 'be a marker of social and economic disadvantage at a young age and a cause of further disadvantage, emotional and physical health problems'. Considered in this way, childhood adversity experienced by young people in care may increase the risk of early pregnancy. In addition, the likelihood of further disadvantage may be compounded for parents in and leaving care, whose care status is already associated with increased risk of poor outcomes (Social Care Institute for Excellence, 2004). The absence of official recording and reporting of pregnancy rates for young people in care – despite these increased risks – has been criticised in both the UK and the US, as has the undeveloped nature of early pregnancy and parenthood prevention initiatives specifically targeted at this group (Svoboda et al 2012; Craine et al 2014; Centre for Social Justice 2015). As such, it is unknown whether progress has been made with respect to reducing the risk of teenage pregnancy for young people in and leaving care, or whether the trends for the population as a whole, are applicable to this group.

In the absence of official statistics related to sexual health outcomes and conceptions for young people in and leaving care, the Voices study sought to explore both if and why this group faced increased risk of early pregnancy and parenthood. Secondary analysis was conducted on survey data collected through the School Health Research Network (SHRN) to investigate whether young people in state care in Wales experience poorer outcomes with respect to sexual health and development. In addition, qualitative data generated with social care professionals in Wales (phase three of the Voices study) explored perceptions of support provision for young people in state care with respect to sexual health and pregnancy prevention.

Methods and results

SHRN Health and Wellbeing Survey

Secondary analysis was conducted on data sets from the 2015 and 2017 SHRN Health and Wellbeing Survey. SHRN is a network of all the secondary schools in Wales who have joined together with researchers, the Welsh government and other organisations to support young people's health (see www.shrn.org.uk). The biennial Health and Wellbeing Survey is completed by secondary school pupils from across Wales and is designed to increase our understanding of risk factors for health, and to help schools and other stakeholders to improve the lives of young people in Wales. The survey provides a range of information with respect to healthy eating and physical activity, mental and emotional health and wellbeing, smoking, alcohol consumption and substance use, as well as sexual behaviour and experience of relationships. The survey offers a valuable opportunity to consider reports directly from young people about their sexual behaviour, and to compare and contrast the answers given by young people in care and non-care settings. While incidences of pregnancy are not available from the data, young people's answers nevertheless provide important insights with regard to risk of unplanned and early pregnancy.

At the time of the 2015 survey, 87 secondary schools in Wales participated and this included schools from each of the 22 local authority areas. A total of 35,187 young people completed the survey. Students were asked who they lived with, with options of 'mother', 'father', 'step mother', 'step father,' 'foster mother', 'foster father', or 'other'; 310 students identified themselves as living in foster care. The research team categorised students as living with 'both parents', a 'single mother', a 'single father', in a 'step family', or in 'foster arrangements'. This data set did not allow for all young people in care to be identified. It is likely that young people living in kinship and residential placements were captured within the category of 'other', but as we could not be certain we focused only on young people in foster care and drew comparisons with young people living in a range of private households.

The analysis was replicated with data from the 2017 survey. During this round of data collection, 193 secondary schools participated, again with representation from all 22 local authorities in Wales. A total of 112,045 young people completed the survey. On this occasion, the range of living arrangements was expanded to include those from the 2015 survey already identified, as well as residential care, kinship arrangements or those living independently. As such, the analysis allowed for young people in kinship arrangements, foster care and residential care to be identified. Young people were identified as living in kinship arrangements if they lived with either their grandparents, aunts/uncles or adult siblings without their birth parents or step parents. It is important to note that, for young people living in kinship arrangements, it was not possible to establish further details of these situations, such as whether young people were living with relatives under a legal order, whether arrangements were agreed and supported by the local authority and defined as formal or informal kinship care, or whether young people were currently or previously 'looked after'. It is possible that corporate parenting responsibilities existed for some, but not all, young people living with relatives other than their parents. Data for young people in kinship arrangements is included in the following discussion; however, young people in this category are not collectively referred to as being 'in care'.

Both surveys asked students aged 11–18 if they had ever sent someone a sexually explicit image of themselves, and whether anyone else had ever sent, forwarded or shared a sexually explicit image with other people without their consent. Students aged 15 and over were asked if they had ever had sexual intercourse. Young people who answered 'yes' to having had sex were also asked questions on their contraceptive use and age at first intercourse.

Results

The results of the analyses are detailed in Tables 2.1, 2.2, 2.3 and 2.4. Key findings from the 2015 survey included:

- Just over 1 in 4 (26 per cent) young people in foster care reported sending a sexually explicit image at least once. This compared to 7 per cent of young people living with both parents, 10 per cent with single parents and 14 per cent of young people in step-parent families. Likewise, approximately 1 in 5 (20 per cent) young people in foster care reported having an image forwarded without their consent. This compared with approximately 1 in 10 (10 per cent) young people living with single or step-parent families and 3 in 50 (6 per cent) young people living with both parents.

Table 2.1: Prevalence of sexual health behaviours by living arrangement 2015

Living arrangement % (n)	Both parents (n = 20,246)	Single mother (n = 5,797)	Single father (n = 798)	Step family (n = 4,055)	Foster parent (n = 310)	Other (n = 490)
Ever sent a sexually explicit image						
More than once	4.4 (863)	7.2 (397)	5.0 (38)	8.4 (327)	20.3 (57)	20.0 (90)
Once	2.7 (537)	4.2 (231)	4.1 (31)	5.1 (200)	5.7 (16)	6.7 (30)
Never	92.9 (18,219)	88.7 (4,917)	91.0 (692)	86.5 (3,366)	74.0 (208)	73.4 (331)
Ever had a sexually explicit image forwarded						
Yes	6.2 (1,217)	9.1 (508)	11.0 (83)	10.3 (405)	19.9 (56)	19.9 (91)
No	93.8 (18,422)	90.9 (5,070)	89.0 (673)	89.7 (3,513)	80.1 (225)	80.1 (367)
Ever had sexual intercourse						
Yes	26.5 (925)	35.2 (380)	34.6 (53)	41.2 (306)	65.0 (39)	60.7 (71)
No	73.5 (2,567)	64.9 (701)	65.4 (100)	58.8 (436)	35.0 (21)	39.3 (46)
Within those who have responded 'yes' to ever had sexual intercourse	(n = 925)	(n = 380)	(n = 53)	(n = 306)	(n = 39)	(n = 71)
Age of first intercourse						
11 years or younger	2.4 (22)	4.3 (16)	2.0 (1)	2.0 (6)	46.2 (18)	23.6 (16)
12 years	0.9 (8)	1.3 (5)	4.0 (2)	3.4 (10)	2.6 (1)	1.5 (1)

Table 2.1: Prevalence of sexual health behaviours by living arrangement 2015 (continued)

Living arrangement % (n)

13 years	4.6 (42)	8.3 (31)	4.0 (2)	10.5 (31)	7.7 (3)	13.2 (9)
14 years	18.9 (171)	25.0 (93)	25.4 (13)	23.3 (69)	12.8 (5)	25.0 (17)
15 years	38.2 (346)	34.9 (130)	35.2 (18)	39.2 (116)	20.5 (8)	23.5 (16)
16 years	25.6 (232)	19.6 (73)	21.6 (11)	18.0 (53)	10.3 (4)	11.8 (8)
17 years or older	8.6 (78)	6.4 (24)	5.9 (3)	3.4 (10)	0.0 (0)	1.5 (1)
Contraception at last intercourse						
Condom						
Yes	52.8 (477)	43.2 (158)	54.0 (121)	40.5 (121)	23.1 (9)	30.0 (21)
No	43. (388)	52.5 (192)	36.0 (18)	56.5 (169)	61.5 (24)	60.0 (42)
Don't know	4.2 (38)	4.4 (16)	10.0 (5)	3.0 (9)	15.4 (6)	10.0 (7)
Birth control pill						
Yes	39.0 (355)	45.4 (169)	42.3 (22)	49.3 (148)	13.5 (5)	38.6 (27)
No	54.5 (497)	48.4 (180)	50.0 (26)	45.0 (135)	64.9 (24)	55.7 (39)
Don't know	6.6 (60)	6.2 (23)	7.7 (4)	5.7 (17)	21.6 (8)	5.7 (4)
Long Acting Reversible Contraception (LARC)						
Yes	15.2 (138)	19.1 (70)	13.5 (7)	21.7 (65)	8.1 (3)	20.6 (14)
No	76.3 (692)	74.1 (272)	75.0 (39)	67.9 (203)	75.7 (28)	64.7 (44)

(continued)

Table 2.1: Prevalence of sexual health behaviours by living arrangement 2015 (continued)

	Living arrangement % (n)					
Don't know	8.5 (77)	6.8 (25)	11.5 (6)	10.4 (31)	16.2 (6)	14.7 (10)
Emergency contraception						
Yes	6.9 (63)	10.3 (38)	8.0 (38)	8.0 (24)	8.1 (3)	12.9 (9)
No	86.4 (788)	85.6 (316)	80.0 (40)	81.0 (243)	75.7 (28)	77.1 (54)
Don't know	6.7 (61)	4.1 (15)	12.0 (6)	11.0 (33)	16.2 (6)	10.0 (7)
Other						
Yes	19.7 (178)	23.4 (86)	24.5 (12)	19.9 (60)	18.9 (7)	16.9 (12)
No	74.1 (668)	72.0 (265)	69.4 (34)	71.8 (216)	73.0 (27)	74.7 (53)
Don't know	6.2 (56)	4.6 (17)	6.1 (3)	8.3 (25)	8.1 (3)	8.5 (6)

Note: Participants who did not respond or reported 'do not want to answer' are not included in the table data.

Table 2.2: Odds ratios for the association between foster care and sexual health behaviours

	Number included in model	Foster care
Ever sent sexually explicit image	n = 30,050	3.63 (2.77–4.78)
Ever had a sexually explicit image forwarded	n = 3,012	3.11 (2.36–4.11)
Ever had sexual intercourse	n = 5,523	4.25 (2.47–7.29)
Age of first intercourse	n = 1,661	-2.00 (-2.54–1.45)
No condom use at last intercourse[a]	n = 1,625	3.12 (1.70–5.76)
No pill use at last intercourse[a]	n = 1,668	4.72 (1.97–11.28)

Note: 95% confidence intervals. All p values are <0.001.
[a] No categories include 'don't know' responses.

- In comparison to young people living with parents and step parents, those in foster care were significantly more likely to report ever having had sexual intercourse. Overall, 65 per cent of young people in foster care reported having had sexual intercourse, compared to approximately 26 per cent of young people living with both parents, 35 per cent living with single parents and 41 per cent living in step-parent families.
- For young people who reported having had sexual intercourse, those living with parents and step parents were most likely to report this first occurring at age 15. In contrast, almost half of young people in foster care (46 per cent) reported this experience at 11 or younger. Such disparity should be considered reflective of experiences of abuse and adversity, as opposed to young people consenting to such experiences.
- Young people in foster care were least likely to report using Long Acting Reversible Contraception or LARCs (such as the contraceptive implant or coil) at last intercourse. Just 8 per cent reported use of LARCs whereas percentages ranged between 14 per cent (living with single father) and 22 per cent (living with step family) for young people living with parents and step parents.
- Young people in foster care were approximately three times more likely to report not using a condom at last intercourse. Nearly a quarter (23 per cent) of young people in foster care reported using a condom, in comparison with 41 per cent in step-parent families, 43 per cent living with single mothers, 53 per cent living with both parents and 54 per cent living with single fathers. Similarly, those in foster care were almost five times more likely to report not using the

contraceptive pill at last intercourse. Just 14 per cent of young people in foster care reported use of the contraceptive pill, while for those living with parents and step parents this was around 40 per cent.

In 2017 a more nuanced analysis was possible given the more detailed data collected about pupils' living arrangements, and findings with respect to young people living in kinship arrangements, foster care and residential settings were highlighted.

Key findings from the 2017 survey included:

- Rates of children living with parents and step parents who reported having sent a sexually explicit image at least once ranged from 10 per cent (living with both parents) to 18 per cent (living with single fathers). In comparison, for young people living in kinship arrangements, the figure was 21 per cent, for those in foster care 20 per cent and for those living in residential care 39 per cent. Reports of having a sexually explicit image forwarded without consent ranged from 13 per cent (living with both parents) to 21 per cent (living with single fathers) for young people living with parents and step parents. For those living apart from parents, the figures ranged from 20 per cent (kinship settings and foster care) to 44 per cent (residential care).
- Consistent with the 2015 data, young people not living with parents were more likely to report having had sexual intercourse. A total of 29 per cent of young people in foster care, 32 per cent in kinship settings and 54 per cent in residential care reported having had sexual intercourse. For young people living with parents and step parents these figures ranged between 17 per cent (living with both parents) to 26 per cent (living with single father).
- The age at which young people were most likely to report having first sexual intercourse was 14 for those living with single fathers and 15 for those living with both parents, single mothers and step families. Young people in kinship and foster care settings were most likely to report this experience happening at age 14, but for young people in residential care, this was most frequently reported at age 11 or younger. These findings could be considered as indicative of childhood abuse and adversity.
- Rates of condom use at last intercourse ranged from 43 per cent (living with single father) to 50 per cent (living with both parents) for young people living with parents or step parents. Lower rates of condom use were reported for young people in kinship arrangements and foster care (40 per cent). Significant disparity was again evident

for those in residential care where only 15 per cent reported using a condom at last intercourse.
- Use of the contraceptive pill at last intercourse was reported by approximately 35 per cent of all young people living with parents and step parents. Interestingly, this was 40 per cent for young people in kinship settings, but contraceptive pill use was lower for those in foster care (26 per cent) and residential care (9 per cent).
- Almost 1 in 5 young people in kinship settings (19 per cent) and 1 in 4 in foster care (25 per cent) reported use of LARCs. This was higher than the rate reported by young people living with parents and step parents, where rates ranged between 11 per cent (living with both parents) and 18 per cent (living with single fathers). This figure was 14 per cent for young people in residential care.
- Young people in residential care (17 per cent) were most likely to report having used emergency contraception. This was followed by young people living with single fathers (15 per cent), those in foster care (13 per cent), kinship arrangements (12 per cent), single mothers (10 per cent), both parents (9 per cent) and step families (8 per cent).
- Combining results for young people living in foster and residential care settings showed them to be twice as likely to report having had sexual intercourse, and twice as likely to report not having used a condom or contraceptive pill at last intercourse.

The findings of the 2015 and 2017 surveys provide valuable evidence in relation to the sexual health outcomes for young people. Findings from the 2017 survey also suggested increased vulnerability for young people living with single fathers and those living in kinship arrangements with relatives other than their parents (some of whom are likely to be 'looked after'). While these results require further consideration, it is the outcomes for young people in care that are the particular focus of this book.

Considered as a whole, the findings highlight increased inequality for care-experienced young people with respect to sexual health outcomes. The findings are consistent with a US evidence review highlighting the potential for earlier and more risky sexual behaviours (Winter et al 2016) and offer little reassurance that disparities in teenage pregnancy rates for young people in care would not be again visible if Craine et al's (2014) health audit were to be repeated.

It is important to note that the findings suggest some improvement in results between 2015 and 2017. It is unclear whether these improvements are an anomaly, indicative of more accurate results due to the larger sample or are reflective of improved policy and practice.

Table 2.3: Prevalence of sexual health behaviours by living arrangement 2017

Living arrangement % (n)	Both parents (n = 62,377)	Single mother (n = 16,120)	Single father (n = 2,111)	Step family (n = 9,712)	Kinship arrangements (n = 1,279)	Foster parent (n = 620)	Residential or children's home (n = 161)
Ever sent a sexually explicit image							
More than once	6.5 (3,914)	9.2 (1,409)	11.3 (226)	10.5 (972)	14.4 (173)	15.5 (90)	29.3 (44)
Once	3.5 (2,080)	4.6 (700)	6.2 (123)	5.8 (533)	6.1 (73)	4.8 (28)	10.0 (15)
Never	90.1 (54,263)	86.2 (13,215)	82.5 (1,648)	83.8 (7,760)	79.5 (955)	79.7 (464)	60.7 (91)
Ever had a sexually explicit image forwarded							
More than once	6.8 (3,020)	9.5 (1,049)	11.3 (161)	10.7 (762)	12.2 (109)	12.2 (50)	32.4 (35)
Once	5.7 (2,540)	7.0 (771)	9.5 (136)	7.2 (515)	7.6 (68)	8.1 (33)	11.1 (12)
Never	87.5 (38,834)	83.5 (9,196)	79.2 (1,130)	82.1 (5,841)	80.3 (719)	79.8 (327)	56.5 (61)
Within those who were asked about sexual intercourse (grades 9–13)	(n = 27,015)	(n = 7,325)	(n = 1,016)	(n = 4,488)	(n = 587)	(n = 273)	(n = 68)

Table 2.3: Prevalence of sexual health behaviours by living arrangement 2017 (continued)

	Living arrangement % (n)					
Ever had sexual intercourse	(n = 4,561)	(n = 1,681)	(n = 1,166)		(n = 190)	(n = 37)
Yes	16.9 (4,561)	23.0 (1,681)	26.1 (265)	26.0 (1,166)	32.4 (190)	29.3 (80)	54.4 (37)
No	83.1 (22,454)	77.1 (5,644)	73.9 (751)	74.0 (3,322)	67.6 (397)	70.7 (193)	45.6 (31)
	Within those who responded 'yes' to ever had sexual intercourse					
	(n = 4,561)	(n = 1,681)	(n = 265)	(n = 1,166)	(n = 190)	(n = 80)	(n = 37)
Age at first intercourse							
11 years or younger	5.2 (224)	7.2 (116)	10.4 (26)	5.0 (56)	10.8 (19)	24.3 (18)	71.4 (25)
12 years	2.4 (106)	3.5 (57)	6.0 (15)	4.1 (46)	5.7 (10)	5.4 (<5)	2.9 (<5)
13 years	11.9 (517)	15.0 (241)	14.5 (36)	15.8 (177)	20.5 (36)	25.7 (19)	2.9 (<5)
14 years	23.6 (1,024)	27.6 (445)	24.5 (61)	26.0 (291)	29.0 (51)	27.0 (20)	11.4 (<5)
15 years	29.7 (1,290)	29.3 (473)	24.5 (61)	32.3 (361)	23.3 (41)	13.5 (10)	5.7 (<5)
16 years	19.8 (860)	12.4 (200)	12.9 (32)	13.0 (145)	9.1 (16)	1.4 (<5)	2.9 (<5)
17 years or older	7.4 (321)	5.0 (81)	7.2 (18)	3.8 (43)	1.7 (<5)	2.7 (<5)	2.9 (<5)
Contraception at last intercourse							
Condom							
Yes	50.4 (2,182)	43.7 (692)	43.4 (108)	46.3 (518)	39.9 (71)	39.7 (31)	14.7 (5)
No	44.8 (1,940)	51.3 (811)	49.4 (123)	49.4 (553)	52.3 (93)	47.4 (37)	67.7 (23)

(continued)

Table 2.3: Prevalence of sexual health behaviours by living arrangement 2017 (continued)

	Living arrangement % (n)							
Don't know	4.8 (209)	5.0 (79)	7.2 (18)	4.4 (49)	7.9 (14)	12.8 (10)	17.7 (6)
Birth control pill							
Yes	35.1 (1,541)	35.2 (564)	34.8 (87)	36.0 (407)	39.6 (72)	25.6 (20)	8.6 (<5)
No	56.6 (2,482)	58.2 (934)	53.2 (133)	56.6 (640)	52.8 (96)	65.4 (51)	74.3 (26)
Don't know	8.3 (362)	6.6 (106)	12.0 (30)	7.4 (84)	7.7 (14)	9 (7)	17.1 (6)
Long Acting Reversible Contraception (LARC)							
Yes	11.2 (487)	14.9 (238)	17.8 (44)	15.0 (169)	19.3 (34)	24.7 (19)	14.3 (5)
No	76.5 (3,321)	72.3 (1,159)	69.2 (171)	73.8 (832)	65.3 (115)	62.3 (48)	68.6 (24)
Don't know	12.3 (534)	12.9 (207)	13.0 (32)	11.3 (127)	15.3 (27)	13.0 (10)	17.1 (6)
Emergency contraception							
Yes	9.0 (393)	9.7 (156)	14.6 (36)	8.4 (95)	11.9 (21)	12.8 (10)	17.1 (6)
No	81.8 (3,569)	80.9 (1,300)	76.5 (189)	83.5 (945)	77.4 (137)	71.8 (56)	68.6 (<5)
Don't know	9.2 (403)	9.4 (151)	8.9 (22)	8.1 (92)	10.7 (19)	15.4 (12)	14.3 (5)
Other							
Yes	19.1 (830)	20.0 (320)	21.1 (53)	19.3 (217)	18.7 (33)	22.4 (17)	11.8 (<5)
No	72.6 (3,161)	72.2 (1,156)	69.3 (174)	73.2 (824)	70.1 (124)	70.0 (53)	73.5 (25)
Don't know	8.4 (364)	7.9 (126)	9.6 (24)	7.6 (85)	11.3 (20)	7.9 (6)	14.7 (5)

Table 2.4: Odds ratios for the association between being in care and sexual health behaviours

	Number included in model	In foster or residential care
Ever sent a sexually explicit image	n = 87,575	2.46*** (2.04–2.97)
Ever had a sexually explicit image forwarded	n = 59,396	.62** (.45–.85)
Ever had sexual intercourse	n = 40,185	2.19*** (1.76–2.73)
Age at first intercourse	n = 7,432	-1.06*** (-2.06–1.29)
No condom use at last intercourse[a]	n = 7,394	1.95** (1.29–2.95)
No pill at last intercourse[a]	n = 7,483	2.13** (1.28–3.54)

Note: 95% confidence intervals. *p value < .0.5, **p value <.01. ***p value < .001.
[a] No values include 'don't know' responses.

In the absence of sustained analysis, such questions remain difficult to answer. Nevertheless, both surveys indicate young people in care to be at increased risk of poor sexual health outcomes, findings that are difficult to comprehend given that these young people are known to professionals and carers, and their support needs routinely assessed and reviewed. The following section draws on interview data from social care professionals to help further understand the reasons for such findings.

Findings from the Voices study

The Voices study also collected primary data from social care and health professionals, all of whom had experience of supporting young people in and leaving care across Wales. This phase was designed to explore professionals' experiences in relation to early pregnancy and parenthood for care-experienced young people (see Chapter 1). The semi-structured interviews sought information about local practice and initiatives designed to ensure sexual health support and prevent early and unplanned pregnancy.

Interviews were conducted with professionals from each of the 22 local authorities (LA) in Wales. Each authority was asked to nominate an individual or individuals; those who took part mainly consisted of team managers with responsibility for children in and/or leaving care, but also included a senior manager, social workers, personal advisers and a 'looked after children's' nurse. Of the 22 interviews, 18 were conducted with one respondent, 3 interviews were conducted with two respondents and 1 with three respondents. All interviews took place within the respondent/s' place of work during 2016. The analysis of the interview data identified key themes in relation to the capacity and capability of the care system to ensure sexual health advice and support for young people.

The system has it covered: professional confidence in available support and expertise

In contrast to the findings of the survey data, professional respondents frequently referred to the strengths of the care system and highlighted its capacity to identify and respond to young people's sexual health needs. This included the statutory protocols and procedures that were in place to assess and review young people's needs (including those with respect to sexual health and relationships), the range of professionals and carers connected to young people who were able to offer help and support in this area, as well as local initiatives designed to engage and respond to young people's needs.

Repeated references were made to the procedures and recording obligations which ensured regular consideration of young people's health needs, including those related to sexual health and contraception. All of the professionals discussed Pathway Plans: the statutory planning process designed to ensure full consideration of young people's needs as they leave care. For example:

> 'Sexual health, contraception, knowledge of sexual health clinics, it's all covered as part of the pathway planning process.' (Senior practitioner LA 18)

> 'The Pathway Plan asks whether or not they are aware of, or have access to sex education, they know how to access birth control ... we make sure that they have been told about it, they've learnt about it at school, the "looked after" nurse has been out to see them.' (Team manager LA 9)

There was broad agreement that supporting young people with regard to sexual health and contraception was shared among the various professionals working with the young person. In particular, residential workers and foster carers were recognised as key sources of support for young people. As noted by one team manager: "ideally the carers will do it in a natural environment" (LA 4) as this would more closely resemble the support ordinarily provided within families. Yet while carers were recognised as important figures, they were not singled out as having primary responsibility for sexual health. Rather, carers, personal advisers and social workers were all seen as well placed to engage young people in discussions regarding relationships, sexual health and contraception:

> 'Within our residential work, residential workers are trained up to [discuss] sexual health with our young people and I'd like to say that all our social workers and personal advisers sort of do that within their role. … I'd like to think that that's always covered in core assessments and just general sort of social work.' (Team manager LA 2)

> 'We do expect the carers, whether they be foster carers or residential staff, to address, work with them, but the social workers obviously have got a responsibility to be talking about the sexual health and, you know, ways to prevent pregnancy but also safe sex.' (Team manager LA 4)

> 'Personal advisers do it [discuss sexual health and development issues] and the social workers. … [I]t's part of our general informal conversations that you tend to have in that relationship-building period with the kids as well, you know, "Oh, how is so-and-so", "Oh you better be safe", you know, "Do you want to talk about that?", "Do you have a plan?", you know, "Have you got contraception?", "Do you want support with that?" or "Would you prefer us to have a conversation with your foster carer?" They're the type of things that we do quite routinely I'd say.' (Senior practitioner LA 1)

In addition, the looked after children's nurse was viewed as an important resource, able to offer specialist knowledge and confidential advice:

> '[The nurse] goes out as part of her role to speak to them when they sort of hit, sort of, well, before puberty, whatever level we feel it is and does some sort of workbooks with them, does discussions with them and does it on whatever level she recognises their development to be. She will support them going to clinics you know and, and do whatever she feels that you know they want to do about

contraception and knowing that sort of stuff.' (Senior practitioner LA 7)

'[The nurse] takes them to clinic, she takes them, she reminds them when things need to be done. And yeah she is very experienced in obviously promoting safe sex etcetera.' (Team manager LA 11)

'I suppose the first and the most important person we have is the "looked after children's" nurse. ... [T]hey'll get all the review documentation and if they pick up on any issues that relate to sort of health and sexual health then, you know, they pick it up and run with it.' (Senior practitioner LA 5)

Professionals described a range of local approaches and initiatives designed to ensure young people's needs were met. Examples included the use of the crying dolls, outdoor pursuits and activities designed to boost self-esteem, information and discussion sessions, as well as outreach and fast-tracked sexual health appointments.

'We have a link with one of the sexual health sort of nurses or workers within the clinic down in the hospital ... so we can sort of fast-track appointments for like contraceptive and sort of try and make it more comfortable and more anonymised for our young people.' (Senior practitioner LA 1)

'We have ... a sexual health worker and we work very closely with her. ... [S]he can access the, she is not a nurse but she can access the GUM [genito-urinary medicine] clinic with the young people, she can set up appointments. She is like absolutely stupendous, you know, we can just phone her up one week and she'll go and visit the next week. She does a lot of healthy relationship work with the young person as well. She does the baby, ah, you know, she organises that you know the baby thing [crying doll].' (Senior practitioner LA 3)

As illustrated by the data presented in this section, there was variety in the support available across different areas and professionals commonly described attempts to engage, inform and advise young people with respect to sexual health and contraception. It is important to note that professional confidence in the potential of the system to meet the sexual health and development needs of young people, is somewhat at odds with the survey findings presented earlier. While the interview findings suggest collective responsibility for the provision of sexual health advice and support, previous research has shown some carers to be unclear and/or uncomfortable about their responsibilities (Corylon and McGuire 1999; Knight et al 2006) and also highlighted that shared responsibility has the potential to diffuse or dilute individuals' sense of duty (Chase et al 2009; Constantine et al 2009; Hyde et al 2016). Moreover, professionals in this study also identified potential reasons for support not reaching or being accepted by young people.

Threats to the effectiveness of the system

Despite respondents' confidence in the potential of the care system to recognise and respond to young people's sexual health needs, a series of threats were acknowledged that were seen as having the potential to undermine its effectiveness. These included the impact of limited or reduced resources, anxieties regarding 'responsible' corporate parenting, as well as the challenges of influencing the individual choices and behaviours of young people.

Limited resources

Several respondents complained about funding cuts and austerity measures which impacted on service provision. Describing pregnancy prevention initiatives within the area, one respondent noted: "I'm not quite sure if that's changing. … [E]verything always is in flux and, you know, with cutbacks things change" (Senior practitioner LA 5). Similarly, describing the impact of funding and organisational restructuring, senior practitioner (LA 16) stated:

> 'We used to do like a drop-in day … we would do an open day, we'd talk about sexual health in the morning and then we'd go and do an activity in the afternoon … but we haven't done it for over a year or so. … [I]t's [because of] funding stopping and just not having the time. … There was a time when it was regular but at the minute everything is up in the air because it's all changed, everyone is bogged down, we're not having these event days …'

Related to this, a personal adviser commented: "The [looked after children's] nurse has run a few sort of courses with the dolls and things ... but I'm not aware that's happened for a while now ..." (LA 20). Other respondents also raised concerns about the limited availability and capacity of looked after children's nurses, including restricted access or shared resources with neighbouring authorities. Reflecting on the impact of such changes to her role, the looked after children's nurse who participated in the research acknowledged this had reduced the support she could provide to individual young people: "until recently, you know, I would physically support young people in going to youth advisory clinics for implants" (LA 10). These findings correspond with those of a survey of looked after children's nurses which also highlighted concerns with respect to capacity within the role to provide specialist sexual health advice and support (RCN 2015).

These accounts highlight the importance of adequate resources in ensuring that young people are well supported with regard to sexual health and pregnancy prevention. In a context of austerity and ever increasing financial pressures on local authorities, these comments from professionals suggest that both the services and individual support available to young people has diminished. This corresponds with a survey of foster carers in the UK which highlighted carers' concerns regarding reduced contact between children and social workers, as well as reduced access to early intervention services (The Fostering Network 2016). In addition, simply being directed to sexual health advice and support is unlikely be the experience of young people in responsible caring families. Viewed in this way, there should be an expectation that professionals and carers are available to literally and/or figuratively hold a young person's hand when accessing sexual health advice and support. While it should be possible for young people to say they do not wish to receive such support, it should not be acceptable that such support is no longer possible due to financial constraints.

'Responsible' corporate parenting

Concerns about being 'good' or 'responsible' corporate parents were also discernible from the interview data. Two practice dilemmas were evident in relation to when young people should be offered sexual health advice, as well as how to respond when sexual health support was needed but when a young person was under the age of consent.

Professionals questioned when young people should be provided with sexual health information and advice. Some felt it was important to treat young people as individuals and offer such advice when it was appropriate and needed. There was a concern not to introduce young people to issues related to sex and relationships before they were ready, and to avoid practice that could unwittingly stigmatise or label young people. However, such efforts also had the potential to leave young people unprepared and unsupported when they started having romantic or sexual relationships. As noted by one respondent: "ideally it's addressed from a younger age but I think quite often in reality what happens is we wait until they become perhaps sexually active before we tend to address" (Team manager LA 4).

Several participants also discussed experiences of working with young people who were known or suspected of being sexually active before the legal age of consent. Previous research has highlighted this as an area of uncertainty for professionals due to the lack of organisational policy and guidance (Constantine et al 2009; Hyde et al 2015). Comparable tensions were also evident in the Voices research. Professionals felt uncomfortable ignoring young people's needs, and recognised the increased risk of pregnancy or sexually transmitted infection. However, they were also concerned not to be seen as promoting or condoning engagement in sexual activity before the age of consent, as this could leave them professionally vulnerable, with their actions viewed negatively by senior managers. One respondent stated that managers were "a little bit twitchy if it's someone under 16 with contraception" (Team manager LA 10).

The comments from professionals highlight an important tension between seeking to pre-empt known risks, while at the same time being conscious not to prematurely prompt, encourage or condone early onset of sexual activity.

Individual choice and control

Respondents highlighted the limits of the influence the care system could have over individual choice and behaviour. For example, several respondents differentiated between ensuring young people had the necessary information and advice, and the extent to which young people acted on the information provided:

> 'I'd say they know, their knowledge is quite good ... they seem to be getting the information but actually doing something about it or using something [contraception], not that good.' (Senior practitioner LA 19)

'For me in my experience when I was a practitioner, it wasn't about young people not knowing about contraception, they know about contraception, it was more about how to initiate the use of that contraception in their relationships. It was more about "I know I should be using contraception or condoms and practising safe sex but I don't know how to insist that happens in the heat of the moment."' (Team manager LA 12)

These quotations emphasise the importance of initiatives aimed at promoting healthy relationships and self-esteem; initiatives which were recognised by professionals quoted earlier as vulnerable as a result of limited or reduced funding.

Professionals also identified a range of individual risk factors which, based on their professional experience, suggested young people were more likely to experience early pregnancy and parenthood. This included young people who were in committed or more serious relationships and were therefore more likely to be sexually active. In addition, professionals felt that young people who experienced disruption and instability in care and/or who were involved in risky sexual behaviour were also at risk of early pregnancy. It is important to consider concerns with respect to young people's wellbeing in the work of Hallett (2016), who noted that young people who feel insufficiently recognised or cared for by protective adults are vulnerable to child sexual exploitation. Likewise, young people with few educational and career aspirations were also deemed to be at increased risk. For example:

'I sort of feel that sometimes with the girls that they haven't got any other aspirations other than to, well, "I might as well have a baby now." ... I don't think they're necessarily planned pregnancies but they're certainly not major sort of shocks ... I think maybe because they haven't got the aspirations to do anything else. It's really sad because there is so much more that they can do but, I mean that's not for everyone but I do, I have sort of thought that with quite a few of them it's just "oh why not get pregnant" kind of thing.' (Team manager LA 2)

'You will talk to some young people and ... at 15 and a half, 16 and you will talk to them and they're already talking about wanting to be a mother ... it was their goal basically to become a young mother and they've been actively trying to be a young mother.' (Senior practitioner LA 3)

The risk factors identified by professionals correspond with those identified in previous research reviews (Connolly et al 2012; Svoboda et al 2012). Similarly, the depiction of some young people, consciously or unconsciously, seeking to fulfil unmet relational needs through sexual relationships and/or early pregnancy and parenthood is consistent with the evidence base, which has long noted the potential for young people to associate parenthood with stability, family, closeness and love (Connolly et al 2012; Svoboda et al 2012):

> 'I think young people who have been through the looked after children system tend to crave those attachments and that family at a younger age, to a higher level, than the general population.' (Team manager LA 13)

> 'I think it's about belonging and attachment and, yeah, wanting to be loved and feel loved, and maybe some sort of sense of belonging and purpose.' (Team manager LA 12)

> 'Yeah I think, for certainly my experience of working with young girls in particular is there can be quite often this idea of loss, bereavement and the urge to become a parent to kind of satisfy that loss … that can certainly be a trigger for pregnancies and certainly repeated pregnancies.' (Team manager LA 14)

> 'I just think sometimes they want someone to love unconditionally, someone that's going to be there. They don't think sometimes of the consequences of that decision making, which is why we try to do that early intervention and that preventative work. And they want that, they want that security in a relationship, somebody is just going to need them unconditionally.' (Senior practitioner LA 1)

These professionals' comments emphasise the influence of young people's experiences before and during care, and suggest that such experiences have the potential to wield powerful influence over individual choice and behaviour, regardless of the provision of sexual health advice.

Discussion: heightened vulnerability and continuing risk of unplanned pregnancy

The findings outlined in this chapter provide valuable contributions to the evidence base with respect to sexual health outcomes and risk of early pregnancy for young people in and leaving care. Despite substantial reductions in teenage conceptions in England and Wales (Office for National Statistics 2017), the findings do little to dispel concerns that young people in care continue to remain at increased risk of early pregnancy and parenthood (Fallon and Broadhurst 2015). The findings illustrate that successes with regard to reduced rates of teenage pregnancy for the general population cannot and should not be assumed to be reflective of trends for young people in care.

The survey data provides new insights about the behaviour and experiences of young people and shows evidence of disadvantage for those with corporate parents. Findings from the 2015 survey highlighted clear disparities for those in foster care, with those young people more likely to report having had sex and less likely to report use of contraception at last intercourse. The additional vulnerabilities of young people in foster care were further highlighted through consideration of digital media, which demonstrated both a higher incidence of sending sexually explicit images, as well as having such images distributed without consent. The consistency of poorer outcomes for young people in foster care compared to young people across the range of households, including two-parent, single-parent and step-parent families exposed the extent of disadvantage.

The increased sample size in the 2017 survey and the ability to identify young people in kinship arrangements, and foster and residential care allowed for a more robust and nuanced analysis. The findings showed some improvements in comparison with the 2015 data but again highlighted poorer outcomes for young people in care. Considered together, young people in foster care and residential care were twice as likely as young people living in other households, to report having had sex and not using condoms or contraceptive pill at last intercourse. Outcomes for young people in residential care were particularly noteworthy and showed evidence of stark disparity in comparison with young people living with parents and relatives, as well as those living with foster carers. Young people in residential care were most likely to have sent and had sexual images forwarded without their consent, most likely to report having had sex, to have experienced this at a younger age and were least likely to have used a condom or been in receipt of the contraceptive pill at last intercourse.

More positively, and in contrast to the 2015 survey data, the 2017 survey showed young people in foster care as most likely to be in receipt of a LARC method of contraception. This is consistent with Public Health Wales (2016) recommendations that care-experienced young people should have access to these forms of contraception. Yet while this increase is to be welcomed, it remains the case that 3 out of 4 young people reported not using LARC. Likewise, only 15 per cent of young people in residential care reported using such methods. Such findings should be recognised as complex and requiring further investigation. For example, while the figures suggest some remedying of previous disadvantage in terms of contraception for young people in foster care (as well as current disadvantage for those in residential care), it would also be important to ward against stigmatising assumptions regarding sexuality and ensure that young people are accessing support which is both wanted and needed.

Interviews with social care professionals provided important practice insights to help understand the survey findings. In contrast to the survey results, professionals expressed some confidence in the care system to identify and respond to young people's sexual health needs. Professionals acknowledged the range of individuals involved with care-experienced young people and pointed to the availability of sexual health knowledge, expertise and support. Rather than considering the system inadequate, interviewees suggested that its effectiveness was undermined by several factors. For example, limited and reduced resources were described as having a direct impact on the services and individual support available to young people. Furthermore, professionals discussed practice dilemmas about when young people could and should be provided with sexual health support and advice. The data suggested some tension between responding to needs of young people and adhering to implicit expectations of senior management. Importantly, professionals also emphasised challenges with respect to influencing young people's choices and behaviours. While information regarding sexual health and pregnancy prevention was available, young people also had to be willing to access and act upon this information.

Conclusion

As highlighted at the outset of the chapter, evidence has long existed about the increased risk of early pregnancy for young people in care (James et al 2009; Mendes 2009; Svoboda et al 2012). Viewed in this way, it is not surprising that the findings reveal poorer sexual health outcomes and include increased reports of sexual intercourse and lower reports of contraception use. Yet it is precisely the context of long-standing international evidence consistently showing care-experienced young people to be at risk, which makes the results so paradoxical; the risks to young people are known, yet needs remain inadequately addressed. Considering the multitude of professionals and carers involved, together with the routine assessment and review of needs, young people in and leaving care could and should have the best and easiest access to sexual health advice and support. However, the findings presented suggest that, rather than combating poor outcomes, the current policy and practice context is unwittingly perpetuating such risks for young people in care. At the national level, the absence of official statistics has enabled this to be an invisible and persistent issue, providing those with corporate parenting responsibilities protection from public scrutiny and accountability. The absence of such scrutiny at national level has enabled sexual health services and provision at local levels to be diminished and left vulnerable to funding pressures. Likewise, underdeveloped guidance, at both national and local level, provides ineffective support and direction to professionals trying to navigate complex ethical dilemmas. Combined with professional acceptance or resignation that early pregnancy will likely be a feature of work with young people in and leaving care, there are multiple barriers inhibiting effective sexual health support for young people in and leaving care. Such provision arguably provides an important foundation, which has the potential to shape young people's experiences and outcomes as parents.

The next chapter continues the focus on outcomes and examines what happens to children born to parents in and leaving care.

Acknowledgements

Tables 2.1 and 2.2 were originally published in Roberts, L., Long, S., Young, H., Hewitt, G., Murphy, S. and Moore, G. (2018) 'Sexual health development for young people in state care: cross-sectional analysis of a national survey and views of social care professionals in Wales', *Children and Youth Services Review*, 89: 281–8.

3

Outcomes for parents in and leaving care: parenting 'success' and corporate parenting failure

Introduction and background

This chapter is concerned with outcomes for young parents in and leaving care. While the increased risk of early pregnancy for young people in and leaving care has been repeatedly evidenced in previous research (James et al 2009), less attention has focused on what happens after young people become parents. This chapter will detail contributions made to this underdeveloped evidence base over the course of the Voices research. The chapter will examine outcomes for parents in and leaving care, and consider whether parents are at increased risk of experiencing compulsory Children's Services intervention and/or separation from their children.

Official statistics in Wales, Scotland and Northern Ireland, currently provide no information with respect to parents in and leaving care (respectively: Information Analysis Directorate 2018; Scottish Government 2018; StatsWales 2018). In England, the annual statistical release reports the number of mothers in care (under the age of 18), a figure which has remained relatively stable at 2 per cent in recent years (Department for Education 2018b). While the availability of such information is helpful when considered against the absence of any details from other UK countries, the English data nevertheless provides limited insights. First, the very low figure of 2 per cent may mask the need for policy and practice attention as it is calculated from the total number of females aged 12 and over. A more meaningful calculation, perhaps, would be to report the percentage of mothers aged between 15 and 17 (a computation not possible from the data released). Likewise, information regarding numbers of fathers does not feature in the reporting, nor is any information available regarding the numbers or proportions of young people who become parents up to the age of 25, while in the process of leaving care and still entitled to statutory support. While information is available in England regarding the numbers of parents aged 17 and 18, not in education, training or employment as a result of pregnancy or parenting commitments (Department for Education 2018b), those who parent and engage with such activities remain unreported.

Considering the limited details with respect to numbers of parents, it is unsurprising that official statistics are unavailable regarding outcomes. Across each of the UK countries, it is unknown how many parents care for their children, with or without formal support, and how many have experienced separation whereby children are cared for by friends and family, local authority or adoptive carers.

Research evidence with respect to parenting outcomes for young people in and leaving care has also been relatively limited. In his review of the literature in 2009, Mendes concluded that "care leavers who became teenage parents are more likely than the general population to come to the attention of child protection authorities" (2009: 14). While Mendes' review noted that studies involving care leaver parents often made fleeting references to parenting outcomes and were typically based on small sample sizes, more recent studies have strengthened the evidence base. Examples include analysis of social work records regarding 2,487 children born to young people in foster care in Illinois between 2000 and 2008. Dworsky's (2015) study found that 39 per cent had been subject to at least one child protection investigation and 11 per cent had spent at least one period in care by age 5. Such outcomes were found to be more likely for younger parents, mothers rather than fathers, those with unstable care experiences and/or had been in care for a shorter time (Dworsky 2015). In Australia, a data linkage study captured 287 care-experienced mothers and their 513 children (Lima et al 2018). The study found almost three quarters of children had been the subject of a child protection notification and 24 per cent were in care. Related to this, findings from a large cohort study in the US, involving 742 care leaver parents aged between 20 and 49, revealed that 9 per cent reported having a child in foster care, compared to a foster care rate of 1.1 per cent in the general population (Foster Jackson et al 2015). In addition, the Midwest Study sought to follow the progress of over 700 young people leaving care across three US states, Iowa, Wisconsin and Illinois. At age 21, 10 per cent of mothers reported as living apart from at least one biological child (Courtney et al 2007), a figure which increased to 17 per cent by age 23/24 (Courtney et al 2009). By age 25/26 19 per cent of mothers reported having at least one child who didn't live with them – over six times the rate for their peers not leaving care. For fathers this figure was 66 per cent and 1.8 times more likely than their peers. Within this developing evidence base, Courtney et al's (2011) report is particularly helpful in providing more detailed insight into the outcomes experienced by parents in and leaving state care. Non-resident children of care leaver mothers were most likely to be living with foster or adoptive parents, whereas children born to care leaver fathers were most likely to be living with the biological mother (Courtney et al 2011).

Less evidence has been available from within the UK. An important text by Elaine Chase and colleagues (2009) which considered pregnancy and parenthood for young people in care highlighted insufficient evidence with respect to outcomes. Some welcome contributions since then include Botchway et al's (2014) survey of 18,492 mothers whose children were part of the Millennium Cohort Study. Findings revealed that, in comparison with mothers who had not been cared for by the state, mothers with a history of care were significantly less likely to live in a high-income household or have achieved a high level of education. They were also more likely to have a baby of low birth weight, be a single parent and experience symptoms of depression. The authors concluded that women with a history of care experience 'carry social disadvantage into motherhood, with the potential of continuing the cycle of deprivation' (Botchway et al 2015: 1). In addition, Freedom of Information requests issued by the Centre for Social Justice (2015) found that 1 in 10 parents in or leaving care aged 16–21 had experienced their own child taken into care within the previous year. Furthermore, analysis of 354 court records for mothers who had experienced multiple care proceedings and removals of children to the care system, found 40 per cent of the women had previously been in care themselves (Broadhurst et al 2017).

Considered cumulatively, individual studies from within and outside of the UK consistently provide evidence of increased vulnerability of care-experienced parents and their risk of poorer outcomes with respect to parenting. While this is valuable in highlighting the importance of policy and practice considerations of pregnancy and parenting for young people in and leaving care, the evidence base remains somewhat piecemeal. At the outset of the Voices study, more evidence relevant to the UK context was needed, including that confirming or contradicting evidence of poorer outcomes, and providing insight into the range of outcomes experienced by parents. In order to do this, secondary analysis of data from the Wales Adoption Study was undertaken to examine the proportions of birth parents identified as care leavers. Adoption is a particularly important consideration in light of the extremity of the intervention and the severance of legal ties between parent and child. In addition, the Voices study collected survey data regarding parents in Wales who were eligible for Children's Services support as a young person 'looked after' or in the process of leaving care. This national 'snapshot' provided insight into the numbers of parents and children, support needs identified for parents as well as current living arrangements for children.

Methods and results

The Wales Adoption Study

Secondary analysis was conducted on data from the Wales Adoption Study. The Wales Adoption Study was concerned with every child placed for adoption by every local authority in Wales between the 1 July 2014 and the 31 July 2015. The Child Assessment Reports for Adoption (CARA) were reviewed by the research team for each of the 374 children captured within this period. For further details of the study and associated findings see Anthony et al (2016). The national data set provided a valuable opportunity to establish how many of the children placed for adoption in the study time period had birth parents who were care leavers. The data also enabled comparison of the information recorded for birth parents identified as care leavers, with that of other birth parents and, similarly, the information recorded about children born to care leaver parents, with that of other children placed for adoption.

Results

The results of the analysis are detailed in Table 3.1. Key findings included:

- Of the 374 CARA files reviewed for Welsh children placed for adoption during the study period, the care status for 356 birth mothers and 240 birth fathers was recorded. Of these, 96 birth mothers (27 per cent) and 45 of birth fathers (19 per cent) were identified as care leavers. Both birth parents were recorded as care leavers for 23 children (6 per cent of the sample).
- For just under a third of care leaver birth mothers (30 per cent) the adoption was with respect to their first child. In these cases, over half of the children were placed in care at birth (58 per cent). For non-care leaver birth mothers, the adoption was with respect to their first child for 51 of the 278 mothers (18 per cent).
- Children who were voluntarily relinquished for adoption accounted for very small numbers in both groups (3 per cent born to care

Table 3.1: Descriptive statistics for study variables by care leaver status of birth parents

	Birth mother				Birth father			
	Care leaver		Non-care leaver		Care leaver		Non-care leaver	
	N	%	N	%	N	%	N	%
Parent characteristics and experiences of adversity								
Childhood physical abuse	46	47.9	76	30.6	19	54.3	47	25.8
Childhood emotional abuse	42	52.6	60	24.3	13	35.1	26	14.4
Childhood sexual abuse	31	32.3	48	19.8	8	22.9	10	5.5
Childhood neglect	61	74.4	81	32.9	23	63.9	35	19.0
Childhood experience of domestic violence	40	48.8	88	36.1	13	37.1	58	32.0
Learning difficulties	35	41.2	73	31.9	24	66.7	38	23.2
Adult mental illness	50	54.9	105	42.0	15	39.5	72	39.3
Adult substance abuse	37	40.7	97	39.6	16	44.4	88	48.4
Adult alcohol abuse	29	33.0	72	30.4	9	25.7	121	65.4
Criminal justice involvement	33	36.3	73	29.2	32	72.7	57	33.5
Child characteristics								
Developmental delay	15	16	48	18.5	11	24.4	37	19.2
Attachment concerns identified by child social worker	11	11.5	46	17.8	8	18.2	33	16.9
Learning difficulties	2	7.4	7	7.1	2	16.7	7	9.9
Low birth weight (<2.5 kg)	10	12.7	22	9.9	4	10.8	20	12.0
Parental appeal of adoption decision	7	9	39	20	3	9	26	18

leaver mothers and 2 per cent born to non-care leaver mothers). However, care leaver mothers were statistically less likely to appeal the adoption than non-care leaver mothers, and low rates of appeal were evident for all care leaver parents (9 per cent of care leaver birth mothers and 9 per cent of care leaver birth fathers appealed compared with 20 per cent and 18 per cent of non-care leaver birth mothers and birth fathers respectively).

- Birth parent experiences of childhood abuse and exposure to violence, including childhood physical abuse, emotional abuse, sexual abuse, exposure to domestic violence in childhood (mothers only) and neglect provided an important distinction between the groups. Care leaver birth mothers were two to five times more likely to have experienced childhood abuse and neglect, while birth fathers who were care leavers were three to seven times more likely to have had such experiences.
- Aside from childhood adversity, relatively few differences were found when comparing the profiles of birth parents and children:
  - There were no significant differences in the age of parents when the child was born or when they were placed for adoption.
  - Two thirds (67 per cent) of birth mothers in the total sample had been known to Children's Services when younger.
  - There were relatively high levels of difficulties for both groups of birth parents with respect to substance misuse, alcohol dependency and criminal behaviour. Analysis of educational achievement, and receipt of welfare benefits were also comparable.
  - Care leaver birth mothers were statistically more likely to be recorded as unemployed and suffer from mental illness.
  - Children born to care leaver parents spent less time on average with them before entering care, but this difference was only statistically significant for fathers.
  - Recordings of abuse or neglect and exposure to domestic violence was high for all children within the cohort, but children born to care leaver parents did not present as statistically more likely to have had suffered such experiences and there were no significant differences regarding birth weight, learning difficulties, development concerns and recorded attachment difficulties.

Survey of local authority leaving-care teams

The Voices study collected primary data from local authorities in Wales. This phase was designed to provide a 'snapshot' of parents who were currently in receipt of or eligible for support from the local authority as a young person in or in the process of leaving care. The design was intended to provide much-needed information regarding the numbers of pregnant and parenting young people in and leaving care in Wales, together with details regarding the range of outcomes experienced by these families.

Twenty out of the twenty-two local authorities participated in this phase of data collection (91 per cent response rate), which spanned twelve months between 2016 and 2017. At the time of data collection, leaving-care support was available to young people up to the age of 21, or 25 if in education, training or employment. While the Welsh government has since committed to supporting all care leavers up to the age of 25 (Welsh Government 2018b), at the time of data collection only a small numbers of parents were identified aged 22–25 (who were in education, training and employment *and* were parents). Similarly, data was unavailable for young people who were parents but who were not eligible for statutory support, as they were not in education, training or employment. As a result of the limited availability of data related to older young people leaving care, the analysis focuses only on parents up to the age of 21.

Local authorities were asked to complete a survey for each parent currently in receipt of statutory support while in care, or in the process of leaving care. Information that would identify the parent such as name, date of birth and address was not requested. Details of pregnancies and births were requested and the survey sought information about outcomes for children. This included details of living arrangements and whether children were subject to any legal orders or in receipt of any local authority support. Information was also sought with respect to recorded needs and risks in relation to parenting, as well as individual needs of the parent. For example, individuals completing the survey were asked to indicate whether young people had ongoing needs in areas including housing, finance, health, education, training and employment; categories informed by statutory guidance detailing key considerations for young people leaving care (Welsh Government 2018c). The survey also requested information about the support available to young people and the formal and informal sources with which they were engaged. An electronic survey tool was used and all data was inputted into SPSS data analysis software.

Results

The results of the analyses are detailed in Tables 3.2, 3.3 and 3.4. Key findings included:

- Surveys were completed with respect to 258 young people who were expecting and/or had at least one biological child. The surveys recorded 238 children, with an additional 44 ongoing pregnancies.
- Of the parents, 206 were female and 52 were male. Their ages ranged between 16 and 21 but the average age of having a baby was 19 years for both males and females.

Table 3.2: Relationship status of parents

		Female N	Female %	Male N	Male %	Total N	Total %
Relationship status	Single	73	35	21	40	94	36
	Relationship (biological parent)	99	47	23	44	122	47
	Relationship (not biological parent)	28	13	5	10	33	13
	Not known	9	4	3	6	9	3

Table 3.3: The number and nature of recorded needs for young people

		Female N	Female %	Male N	Male %	Total N	Total %
Number of recorded needs	0	29	14	7	13	36	14
	1–4 needs	124	60	25	48	149	58
	5 + needs	53	26	20	38	73	28
Recorded needs	Family/relationships	96	15	27	14	123	15
	Mental health	88	14	18	9	106	13
	Housing	79	13	20	10	99	12
	Financial/budgeting	73	12	21	11	94	11
	Education, employment and training	68	11	26	13	94	11
	Domestic abuse	62	10	19	10	81	10
	Independent living skills	59	9	21	11	80	10
	Drug/alcohol misuse	44	7	23	12	67	8
	Other	27	4	18	9	45	5
	Learning difficulty	14	2	3	2	17	2
	Physical health	11	2	3	2	14	2
	Learning disability	2	0	1	1	3	0
	Total	623	100	200	100	823	100

- Parents ranged in the age they came into care, the length of time spent in care and the stability experienced in terms of living arrangements. The majority of parents primarily lived in foster care (73 per cent), followed by residential care (10 per cent), a placement with family or friends (7 per cent) or supported accommodation (5 per cent).

Table 3.4: Living arrangements of children

		Female N	Female %	Male N	Male %	Total N	Total %
Child living arrangement	Care leaver parent (subject of the survey)	139	72	12	24	151	62
	Other biological parent	3	2	23	47	26	11
	Local authority carers	19	10	5	10	24	10
	Adoptive carers	18	9	3	6	21	9
	Friends/family	13	7	5	10	18	7
	Other	1	1	1	2	2	1
	Total	193	100	49	100	242	100

- Around half of the sample (47 per cent) were in a relationship with the other biological parent, 36 per cent were single and 13 per cent were in a relationship with another partner. Of the 258 participants, 12 per cent were recorded as being in a relationship with a care-experienced partner.
- The surveys identified a wide range of support needs (excluding parenting-related needs) for parents. Over the course of data collection, a total of 823 needs were recorded in areas such as relationships, mental health and housing. At least 1 recorded need was identified for 86 per cent of the sample, 58 per cent had between 1 and 4 recorded needs and over a quarter had in excess of 5. The most cited needs for both mothers and fathers were difficulties with families and relationships. For mothers, this was followed by mental health, housing, financial and budgeting, and education, employment and training. For fathers, family and relationship difficulties was followed by education, employment and training, drug and alcohol misuse, independent living skills, and financial and budgeting.
- The majority of children were living with the parent identified in the survey (62 per cent). An additional 11 per cent of children were recorded as living with their other biological parent (see Table 3.4). Of the children living with the parent identified in the survey (n = 151), 15 per cent were subject to a child protection plan or investigation and 19 per cent were receiving some form of voluntary family support through the local authority.
- Over a quarter of children were not living with at least one biological parent. Of these children, 10 per cent were in local authority care, 9 per cent were living with adoptive parents and 7 per cent of children

were being cared for by family or friends. Children separated from mothers were most likely to be living with local authority carers and adoptive parents. Children separated from fathers were most likely to be living with the biological mother followed by local authority and friends/family carers.

- When support needs were considered in relation to where children were living, 45 per cent (n = 342) of needs were experienced by young people living with their children. Nearly half of young people living with their children had physical health, mental health, education, employment and training, domestic abuse, drug and alcohol misuse, learning difficulty, financial/budgeting and family relationship needs. Lower levels of needs were noted for young people where their children were living with the other biological parent (14 per cent), local authority carers (14 per cent), friends or family members (14 per cent) and adoptive carers (13 per cent).

Discussion: resilience in spite of adversity and problematic corporate parent relationships

The findings outlined earlier provide valuable contributions to the evidence base with respect to young people in and leaving care who are parents. Secondary analysis of a national data set, together with survey data completed by all but two local authorities in Wales, enables a comprehensive consideration of needs and outcomes for parents in and leaving care.

It is important to note that the majority of children identified within the Voices study, were living with their care-experienced parent (62 per cent) or other biological parent (11 per cent). The fact is that the majority of parents were actively caring for their children, often in spite of multiple and multifaceted personal needs. In this way it is hoped the findings will be used to champion the parenting potential of young people in care and to recognise tenacity and resilience in the face of adversity of challenge.

Despite these hopes, the findings add further support to the evidence base demonstrating increased rates of intervention and separation for children born to care-experienced parents (Courtney et al 2011; Roberts et al 2017; Wall-Wieler et al 2018). Within the Voices sample, around one in four children (26 per cent) were separated from both parents at the time of data collection; 10 per cent of children were in the care of local authority carers, 9 per cent with adoptive carers and a further 7 per cent living with friends and family. Moreover, for children living with a care-experienced parent, around one in three (34 per cent) were in receipt of some form of statutory intervention. In 2017, official statistics in Wales showed 1 per cent of children in state care (Welsh Government 2018a) and 3 per cent in receipt of care and support (including those 'looked after', on the Child Protection Register and those with a Care and Support Plan) (Welsh Government 2018d). Considered alongside these figures, the stark disparity of outcomes for children born to young people in and leaving care are clear.

Further compounding reasons for concern, care leavers represented over a quarter of birth mothers and almost a fifth of birth fathers within the sample of birth parents whose children were being adopted. When considering outcomes for children born to parents in and leaving care, adoption is particularly important given that the intervention permanently severs the legal ties between a child and their birth family. Typically providing few if any guarantees of ongoing contact, adoption can induce intense feelings of grief and loss for parents (Neil 2006; Memarnia et al 2015; Broadhurst and Mason 2017). Findings that sizeable proportions of birth parents on the receiving end of the highest level of state intervention in family life, had themselves been parented by the state, should warrant immediate policy and practice attention. In addition, findings suggesting that sizeable proportions of care leavers experienced their first child being placed for adoption, including the removal of their child at birth, raises questions about the support and opportunities provided to them as parents. Related to this, it is noteworthy that non-care leaver mothers were statistically more likely to appeal the adoption orders than care leaver mothers. With a powerful and supportive state as parent, it could be argued that care leaver parents would be in the best position to appeal the adoption. However, if their relationship with the state as parent is problematic and access to the necessary resources limited, appeals may be considered futile. Viewed in this way, the findings necessitate further consideration of the relationship between the young person as parent and the state as parent.

As well as problematic outcomes, findings from both the Wales Adoption Study and the Voices survey data highlight multiple and wide-ranging support needs for parents in and leaving care. While high levels of needs and difficulties were present for all birth parents whose children were placed for adoption, care leavers were distinguishable by their childhood experiences of abuse and neglect. Such experiences warranted the admission of these individuals into the care system and, as such, they were visible to professionals; their vulnerabilities, histories and needs were known. There were opportunities to influence their lives and future trajectories.

In addition, survey data encompassing parents both living with and separated from their children, showed only 14 per cent to have no additional needs. Most commonly, parents faced between 1 and 4 support challenges in areas such as relationships, health, housing and independent living skills: areas which fall within the realm of corporate parenting responsibility. Again, these young people have had and continue to have, contact with numerous carers and professionals, with their needs and progress routinely and formally considered. As such, it is deeply problematic that the findings suggest them to be in significant need and with sizeable proportions experiencing poor outcomes. Viewed in this way, it is hard to conceive of these findings as anything other than missed opportunities and corporate parenting failure.

Finally, it is somewhat puzzling that higher levels of support needs were recorded for parents who were caring for their children. Prior to the analysis, it had been anticipated that young people with higher levels of support needs would be those most likely to be separated from their children. In other words, the more parents were struggling with their own needs, the less able they would be to meet the needs of their children. Yet the analysis showed that almost half of young people living with their children had physical health, mental health, education, employment and training, domestic abuse, drug and alcohol misuse, learning difficulty, financial/budgeting and/or family relationship needs. In contrast to notions of 'success', the findings illuminate the potential for ongoing struggle and disadvantage.

Conclusion

To conclude, the findings from the book's first section on outcomes, paint a damning picture of corporate parenting 'success' in ensuring positive trajectories and transitions to parenthood for young people in and leaving care. The findings of this chapter, combined with those presented in the previous chapter, suggest that care-experienced young people continue to face increased risk of early pregnancy compounded by increased risk of compulsory intervention and separation.

The results call into question the ability, capacity and commitment of the corporate parenting system to ward against early, unplanned pregnancy, but also to adequately support young people as parents. As noted in the previous chapter, the findings appear almost incomprehensible considering the range of connected professionals and agencies, and the wealth of resources at their disposal. Arguably, the absence of official statistics has enabled this issue to escape much-needed policy and practice attention.

The following two chapters seek to contextualise findings of poor outcomes, with the reflections of professionals who support young people leaving care, as well as those of care-experienced parents. The next section is intended to personalise the statistics, exploring professionals' perspectives of practice, as well as parents' personal experiences and reflections on their parenting journeys.

Acknowledgements

Table 3.1 was originally published in Roberts, L., Meakings, S., Smith, A., Forrester, D. and Shelton, K. (2017) 'Care leavers and their children placed for adoption', *Children and Youth Services Review*, 79: 355–61. Tables 3.2, 3.3 and 3.4 were originally published in Roberts, L., Maxwell, N. and Elliott, M. (2019) 'When young people in and leaving state care become parents: What happens and why?', *Children and Youth Services Review*, 104: 104387.

4

Professional perspectives: assessing parenting potential and managing dual responsibilities

Introduction and background

This chapter returns to the perspectives of professionals and examines their views and experiences in regards to supporting young people in and leaving care who are parents. Although this book will repeatedly argue that corporate parenting responsibilities are not solely the responsibility of social services, professionals with day-to-day responsibilities for engaging with young people in and leaving care come closest to embodying the corporate parent (Rutman et al 2002). They are also uniquely placed to reflect on the range of needs and experiences of care-experienced parents, as well as providing valuable insight into system responses and support availability. As such, their perspectives offer important contextual detail from which to consider the increased risk of social work intervention and separation for children born to parents in and leaving care.

Previous research with care-experienced parents has typically provided a damning assessment of professional intervention and support. Mantovani and Thomas (2014) noted the potential for parents to face a 'presumed incompetency' with respect to their ability to be parents, while Knight et al's (2006) findings suggested assessments of parents could vary according to the individual social worker and team. Care-experienced young people have reported a mistrust of social workers, perceiving them as interfering and unhelpfully monitoring (Corylon and Maguire 1999; Chase et al 2009). Rather than social workers being providers or facilitators of meaningful support, Haydon (2003) reported parents' perception of being under scrutiny from professionals and judged more harshly because of their care status. Related to this, Rutman et al (2002) observed the potential for assessments of parents to be influenced by middle-class understandings of 'good' parenting and noted a propensity for professionals to perceive intergenerational cycles of care as 'inevitable'.

Despite these criticisms, the potential for positive relationships with professionals has also been noted. Leaving-care professionals can be a key source of support for care-experienced parents (Corylon and McGuire 1999) and as highlighted in Chase et al's (2009) study have the potential to offer valuable practical and emotional support. Nevertheless, challenges inherent in professional roles to support parents in and leaving care are also apparent. For example, Barn and Mantovani (2007) highlight the context of both risk and vulnerability – a salient consideration when thinking about the obligations on leaving-care professionals to support young people as well as adhere to safeguarding responsibilities. Rutman et al (2002) highlighted the potential for 'dual roles' and conflicted responsibilities with regard to safeguarding and support. While Dixon et al (2006) were more positive about the potential to combine the monitoring of risk with supporting and advocating for young people, Rutman et al (2002) pointed to the dominance of risk models and noted an absence of explicit policy with regard to supporting parenting. Likewise, Blazey and Persson (2010) argued that assessing social workers are required to focus on the best interests of the child, considerations which take precedence regardless of the challenged circumstances and disadvantaged histories of the parent.

Findings from the Voices study

The Voices study engaged with leaving-care professionals from across Wales to explore their experiences of working with parents in and leaving care (see Chapter 1). A series of themes emerged which highlighted individual and structural factors, both of which had the potential to influence professional practice. This section first examines professional conceptualisations of the parenting potential of young people in and leaving care. The potential for professionals to have anxieties regarding young people's parenting capabilities, based on both experiences before and during care, is explored. This is followed by a discussion of official policies and expected planning procedures. The potential for young people to be discriminated against and/or disadvantaged within these processes is highlighted, as are the competing tensions faced by leaving-care professionals in seeking to support young people, while also adhering to safeguarding responsibilities. Finally, professional reflections regarding barriers and facilitators to 'successful' parenting are outlined. This includes professionals' assessments of the adequacy of corporate parenting support for parents and the potential for a more proactive and supportive corporate parent and grandparent.

The foundations for parenting success

As discussed in Chapter 2, professionals believed that young people's experiences before and during care had the potential to influence the likelihood of early pregnancy. Over the course of the interviews, similar connections were made with regard to parenting potential. Many professionals expressed anxieties about the impact of previous experiences on young people's capacity to be 'successful' parents:

> 'I mean their experience is going to obviously impact on their ability to parent … most relationships and experiences of parenthood is skewed or is dysfunctional so it's not going to have a good impact.' (Team manager LA 3)

> 'I think young people that have had very negative experiences, awful experiences, really, you know, severe neglect, very poor family relationships and that obviously is going to affect their attachments and their ability to form relationships with others, their ability then to form relationships with their child.' (Senior practitioner LA 20)

> 'I think we tend to parent very similar to how we have been parented. If young people are left in the family home for years and for example if they weren't removed until 12, 13 years of age and they've had poor parenting then they've going to have seen a different pattern to perhaps myself who had parents who were you know full of love and attention and nurturing et cetera.' (Team manager LA 5)

Besides concerns about the impact of experiences prior to care, concerns were also voiced about the impact of experiences while in the care system. For example, one team manager (LA 1) made reference to the 'safer care systems which sometimes prevent people from parenting in a natural way' and mean 'children don't always get role modelled into how to be a parent'. Safer care systems involve foster carers being aware of risk and making adaptations to daily living with the primary aim of making children and young people feel safe and protecting them from further abuse (Slade 2012). However, for the team manager, the practices had the potential to impact on intimacy and relationships, and subsequently have a detrimental effect on young people's responses to and care of their own child.

Adding to concerns about the impact of care experience, another team manager highlighted the impact of changes in carers and homes:

> 'Lots of our children who have been looked after change placements, they have different people looking after them. The ability to understand that their own child is going to need one significant attachment figure or a consistency in life is not something that they've experienced. ... I think, particularly with some of our children that have moved around an awful lot, they may not have witnessed consistency in parenting.' (Team manager LA 16)

The comments highlight the propensity for professionals to question the foundations for young people to be successful parents because of experiences of instability, problematic relationships and insufficient exposure to 'good' parenting. Phrased simply, the idea is that a care-experienced young person didn't experience good parenting, therefore does not know how to be a good parent. While the validity of such assumptions is open to debate, the basis for such reflections is explicable. For example, the reflections are likely informed by practice experience and borne out of professionals' understandings of parents' needs and difficulties. Likewise, they may be understood as logical or common sense; as humans we learn from those around us and our experiences shape how we perceive and interact with the world. The reflections also chime with popular theoretical frames employed within social work such as Attachment Theory (Bowlby 1969; Ainsworth et al 1978; Hazan and Shaver 1987) and Social Learning Theory (Bandura 1977). In recent years, policy and practice has also emphasised the significance of 'parental determinism' and the idea that parents and parenting are primarily responsible for the outcomes and future prospects of children (Furedi 2010). By nature of their care status, young people may be seen – consciously or unconsciously – as lacking or damaged because of the absence of 'good' parenting. Such perceptions will be revisited in the next chapter, but it is important to acknowledge at this juncture that a deficit perception of parenting potential was heavily criticised by young people. Previous experiences of poor or inadequate parenting were typically acknowledged by young people and they were explicit in their wish to do better and be better for their own children.

Despite the propensity to doubt or question parenting capacity because of past experiences, leaving-care professionals also repeatedly championed the parenting successes of care-experienced young people and acknowledged the prevalence of stigma and discrimination. The following section examines professional reflections regarding official procedures and expectations of practice in relation to young people in and leaving care who were pregnant and/or parenting.

Procedures, planning and expectations of practice

Professionals were asked about practice responses to young people in and leaving care who presented as pregnant. Several professionals discussed the potential for young people to be formally referred to Children's Services for a pre-birth assessment. One team manager (LA 3) stated that the local authority policy was to automatically refer every young person for assessment:

> '[Children's Services] open up an initial assessment, proportionate assessments on young people really … it's to offer support more than anything but it's also, you know, their experience of parenting is so, will be so significant on their ability to be a parent, it doesn't mean that they're going to be bad parents but I think we have to try and take that into consideration. … It's not a policy but I think it's, well I have been told by senior managers to do it as well and I was, first of all I was against it but I think it's … you know, you can open it, have a look and then close it, which is fine, but it's about putting the support in there because, as a looked after young person you're not going to have the support networks, necessarily, that other young people would have from families … and it's to put in everything that we can at sort of the earliest stage …'

The team manager acknowledged that this practice was controversial and had caused some disquiet within the team:

> 'There were some people in the team saying "Just because they were looked after I'm not going to refer, when they're pregnant, I'm not going to refer them" and I would say "No, you have to" just because we need to be on top of it, that's more of a support thing not discriminating. … But there are some that there are literally no issues, it's just an open and shut kind of no further action.'

The team manager just quoted was the only professional to openly discuss and attempt to justify the routine referral and assessment of expectant parents. Her response to the uneasiness about the practice within the team was portrayed as a debate between whether referral and assessment constitutes discrimination or proactive efforts to ensure the provision of support. For the team manager, the directive acknowledges the vulnerabilities of young people in and leaving care, and anticipates some additional needs with regard to parenting. As highlighted earlier, there is a propensity to assume that care-experienced young people's parenting potential has been damaged by their experience both prior to and/or during care. In this way, the automatic referral ensures the identification and consideration of support needs at the earliest opportunity. Nevertheless, for other professionals in the team, the standardised approach to refer all young people based on their care status was unnecessary and discriminatory. Supporting this view, the inability of professionals to make a judgement not to refer young people in instances where there were no concerns (and the referral was likely to be 'open and shut') highlights care status, rather than support needs, to be the determining factor in decisions regarding referral. Although not acknowledged within the interview, such a policy is likely indicative of risk-averse practice and efforts to ward off blame and scrutiny in the event of child protection failures. As discussed by Ferguson (2011: 34) 'professional systems have become more and more risk averse' with each decision 'potentially open to public scrutiny and risk laden'. Yet Bilson et al (2017) have also argued that unnecessary investigations are harmful to children and their families, a notion that may be particularly relevant to young people who are dependent on corporate parents.

In other examples, respondents acknowledged an expectation rather than an official directive to refer young people for an assessment:

> '[There is] an unspoken policy of every looked after child needs to be referred.' (Senior practitioner LA 4)

> 'I don't think you'll find it written down anywhere but there's an expectation that they will be referred onto Children's Services as unborn yeah. I don't agree with that because I think each case should be assessed on its own merits but there is ... a blanket expectation that they should all be referred onto Children's Services. ... I think that there is a long-held view that looked after children who become parents will inevitably fail, or struggle, and will need additional services put in.' (Team manager LA 11)

In this example, the team manager rejects the view that routine referral is required to identify and respond to parents' support needs. Rather, the comments imply that the practice is based on stigmatising and generalised views of care-experienced young people. In an effort to resist expectations to make a formal referral to the safeguarding team, one professional respondent discussed how the leaving-care service had opted to undertake their own parenting assessments:

> 'We'll do the [parenting] risk assessment to, that's really to justify why we're not referring. … [W]e use that to, like I say, to justify why we're not referring, because I think some people feel that, well, they're looked after they must have a referral, you know, and I don't think that should be always be the case.' (Personal adviser LA 22)

The comments of the personal adviser again suggest the relevance of risk-averse practice and the need for professionals to evidence and justify decisions. While the practice is arguably well-meaning in its attempt to avoid formal referral, it nevertheless constitutes a distinct and different response based on young people's care status. In this authority, all pregnant and parenting young people supported by the leaving-care team would be subject to an assessment of parenting capacity, which would not routinely be conducted for those not living in care settings. Rather than providing evidence to justify a referral to Children's Services, in this example evidence is being generated to prove why a referral is unnecessary. Outside of this authority, other professionals suggested for care-experienced parents there was an expectation "to prove that someone is good enough, rather than it being a proof that someone isn't good enough" (Team manager LA 8). Such comments again speak to the propensity to doubt or question young people's parenting capacity based on their care status.

In other interviews, leaving-care professionals stated that there was no official policy and there had been a general move away from automatically referring young people for pre-birth assessment. Discussing her relief at the change, the team manager in LA 14 stated: "I have always been a little bit reluctant, if I am honest, to automatically refer young people to Duty and Assessment, because I have felt quite passionately about labelling."

Echoing the disquiet of this team manager, other professionals also considered automatic referrals based on care status to be stigmatising and discriminatory.

'We did [automatically refer] previously. … [T]here used to be a standard accepted process but actually I think that a couple of years ago that was explored and there was a very emotional, sort of very passionate consensus really that that's wrong and that the fact that someone has been looked after doesn't within themselves cause a risk. There are support needs there and that should be investigated, and that can be done through other avenues, that can be done through third sector, that can be done through [the] team around the family or through our own support, but that doesn't equate to a child protection issue.' (Team manager LA 15)

'Just because somebody has gone through the care system, it doesn't make them automatically a bad parent you know there are 16-year-olds, 17-year-olds in the community who have come through whatever type of family but haven't come through the care system, they're not given an automatic pre-birth assessment and I think we really need to move away from that stigma and, you know, because somebody is in care it doesn't make them a bad person.' (Team manager LA 8)

The findings outlined in this section bring into focus important complexities with regard to parents in and leaving care. While there was widespread acknowledgement of the potential for care experience to influence parenting capacity, the majority of professionals objected to practices which treated care-experienced parents as a homogeneous group and failed to recognise individual circumstances and strengths. While some teams were willing and able to challenge stigma and discrimination internally, this was less possible in others where procedural requirements and/or particular expectations of practice dominated. This may be indicative of the quality of relationships social workers have with both managers and peers, and the supportive opportunities for reflection and managing risk (Engstrom 2019).

Despite progression within some leaving-care teams, professionals also acknowledged more widespread stigma. Several participants stated their belief that young people were more likely to come to the attention of Children's Services as they were a 'known name' within the local area. Referring to an example:

'Stigma from previous case workers. I think the case we were talking about earlier you couldn't walk into Children's

Services without a case worker coming to you and telling you everything about why this person shouldn't have a baby and it was, every building you'd walk in, somebody would turn around and go "That person shouldn't look after that baby" and you'd think "This is absolutely none of your business." ... really derogatory comments made that ... she couldn't look after a rat ... that's an extreme case but I think the stigma is a massive one, really big.' (Team manager LA 1)

Similarly, another team manager (LA 16) discussed an example where a child protection referral was made but subsequently closed:

'[E]verything was fine. But it was more, I think it was more about her name was known previously and I think it was more about that. ... I think it was people knew who she was and her name went before her, and I really do think that because [Children's Services] went out and it was nothing, no further action. But how unfortunate is that? There is a stigma.'

In other examples, health professionals were identified as likely to refer care-experienced young people to Children's Services. The following senior practitioner (LA 18) was discussing how the leaving-care team would monitor the situation and decide whether a referral for a pre-birth assessment was necessary but added: "often you get a referral prior to that from Health, we find". Similarly, another senior practitioner commented:

'I had a phone call the other day off a health visitor actually, one of my young people now which I've got no, no issue about her, there's no risks about her pregnancy at all ... if something does happen I'd eat my hat honest to God, you know and the health visitor said "Oh well she is a looked after child so doesn't that mean she needs to be referred immediately?"' (Senior practitioner LA 4)

The comments suggest that care-experienced parents face pervasive stigma and discrimination. There is a propensity to doubt or question care-experienced young people's parenting capacity based on their previous experiences of abuse and/or care. This stigma means that parents can be judged differently to non-care-experienced parents and are more vulnerable to referral to Children's Services. The effects of such stigma may occur at any or multiple points during pregnancy or parenting. For professional agencies, policies or expectations to refer to Children's Services may reflect risk-averse practice and/or the need to prioritise safeguarding responsibilities. The tensions inherent with balancing responsibilities with respect to safeguarding, with duties to support and respond to the needs of care-experienced young people are further explored in the next section.

Disadvantage and dual responsibilities

As well as care-experienced young people being at increased risk of referral to Children's Services, some professionals also felt these young people were disadvantaged when subject to statutory assessments. Several referred to young people being stigmatised because of their care status and felt they needed to advocate on behalf of the young people:

> 'Our personal advisers are very good and they are advocates for the young people. ... I have been to meetings where, you know, professionals who you would have thought should have known better have made comments about care leavers that actually made you feel very uncomfortable. And, you know, I think there is still a degree of discrimination, whereas, you know, you are looking at the individual and the young people who become looked after and accommodated, often the issues are nothing to do with them at all, it's to do with their parenting, you know, how they were parented so how care leavers get the stigma that they've got is, you know, in some ways beyond me.' (Senior practitioner LA 7)

> 'There is sometimes strain between the personal adviser and the social worker doing the assessment ... but I am very clear I think this is what the personal adviser's role is, and if she is there and needs to advocate for that young person with the social worker, that's her role. And, yeah, we have to keep the child, the baby, at the forefront and paramount and all that sort of stuff, but we have to remember this is our child too.' (Team manager LA 10)

These comments suggest that leaving-care professionals are sometimes required to challenge stereotypical judgements about care leavers and their capacity to be parents. Related to this, the relationship between assessing social workers and parents was often seen as key to parents' engagement and participation in the process:

> 'I had one [parent] where she had a change of social worker. … [I]n comparison to the social worker that she had [previously, it] made a massive difference in [her] wanting … to engage in that process. So the avoidance that she was showing was that personality clashing in the early stages, whereas if she had got on with the worker from the onset that wouldn't have been an identified issue.' (Senior practitioner LA 21)

Consistent with this suggestion, Ferguson's (2016) ethnographic study of home visits highlighted varied practitioner skills and relational capacity. Ferguson concluded that where workers were able to communicate and engage positively with families, there was potential for 'deep and meaningful' relationships as well as therapeutic change. Similarly, Wilkins and Whittaker (2018) observed both directive and authoritarian approaches with families, as well as relationship-based and participatory ways of working. Interestingly, the authors noted variation in practice across workers but also in individuals' interactions with different families.

Yet while one senior practitioner (LA 21) emphasised the relationship fit between parent and social worker, more concerning comments were made by the team manager of LA 3:

> 'I might be speaking really out of turn here but I feel sometimes the way the outcome can be … can depend on perhaps, you know, who the social worker is of the unborn or the child, and the team manager, and how that goes because I've had, I've had say two cases that to me have been quite sort of similar in terms of what the needs are, what the risks are, you know, in terms of sort of weighted you know? And one has gone to proceedings and one has a rehab home and I can't quite see the consistency and that really really worries me, that it can be dependent on what social worker has it.'

In Critchley's (2020) study of pre-birth child protection, she noted that intervention decisions were influenced by the extent to which workers were focused on the baby or the family, their previous experiences of negative or tragic outcomes, as well the extent to which they felt vulnerable or supported in their decision making. While the experiences of parents in this study are not limited to pre-birth interventions, it is important to consider the extent to which outcomes and trajectories for young people may be heavily influenced by values, attitudes and approaches at both individual and local levels.

Efforts to advocate on behalf of parents in and leaving care were sometimes interpreted as professionals being naïve or downplaying safeguarding risks. However, this was rejected by leaving-care professionals, who felt they were able to assess situations in terms of risk as well as young people's resilience:

> 'I think sometimes other teams might think we're [seeing the situation through] rose tinted glasses, it's not about that. ... [W]e can see ... the resilience, can't we, in these young people that they won't see. And they will go in and say "Right, well they're in this type of relationship and they've been in care so they've got these problems" and it's like, yeah, and those problems will always exist, but they have been so resilient and actually they can be resilient for that child.' (Team manager LA 13)

Similarly, the team manager quoted next felt that young people were often assessed and judged without appropriate recognition given to the circumstances and challenges parents were coping with:

> 'When I think back, when I had kids that was terrifying and hard enough but I had, you know, [a] partner and I had family and it was really hard, so [I] just look at some of these girls now, on their own in crummy little flats up in [Town A] or whatever with a little one, and I just think my God, they're amazing. But everyone is so quick to just bring them down you know and say "Ah, yeah, but they do this" ... or "But yeah I found that they had smoked cannabis" and I am not condoning that at all but actually, in the scheme of things, they're doing amazing you know?' (Team manager LA 2)

Adding to the potential disadvantaged position of care-experienced parents, some professionals made reference to the wealth of historical information that is held on care-experienced young people:

'The sheer fact we've got so much information on these young people … when you look at some of the chronologies … and you know the way things are sometimes written and I think everybody goes "Oh, this is really scary." … [I]t is a shame because everything they've ever done you know we will know about. … There are some that we don't think there is any risks, no concerns you know, yes, ok, they have behaved stupidly in the past, but how they're presenting now, you know, it's and I think somewhere there has to be a cut-off point doesn't there, of when are we going to stop looking at the behaviours of this person when they were 14 and now they're 19 you know?' (Personal adviser LA 22)

The personal adviser's comments raise the potential for contrasting perceptions of parenting risk and capacity between those with current and/or established relationships with young people and those more reliant on recorded information. Likewise, the senior practitioner quoted next noted the potential of such records to wield powerful influence over social work assessments: "Our bottom line really is 'Would you say that for any other child?' And if the answer is, 'Well actually probably not but we know the history', well that shouldn't be the case then" (Senior practitioner LA 7).

The comments suggest the mere existence of records has the potential to negatively influence assessments and judgements. Comparable information would not be held for parents who have not lived in care settings or been subject to social work intervention during their childhoods, and social workers would be required to assess the family situation based on the presenting information. In such instances it is also unlikely that assessing social workers would seek substantial and in-depth historical information. While it would arguably be negligent of social workers to ignore the wealth of information available to inform assessments of parents in and leaving care, it is important to acknowledge that such records do not provide direct and unbiased accounts but are rather constructions of events which serve a particular purpose (Taylor and White 2001). The extent to which records can be representative of young people's lives and histories is questionable. For example, records are more likely to capture negative or concerning events as opposed to recognising strengths, achievements or simply the everyday and mundane aspects of young people's lives. Moreover, the accuracy of the records may be disputed by young people and the details may have little relevance to young people's current behaviours and demeanours.

The comments quoted portray leaving-care professionals as a key source of support for parents: able to recognise resilience in young people, to champion their rights and to challenge stigma. Yet in other comments, the extent to which leaving-care professionals were able to support and prioritise the needs of young people was less clear. Professionals made reference to dual responsibilities and divided loyalties which inhibited the extent to which they could be supportive to young people. Such issues became apparent when there were concerns about parenting and professionals were balancing responsibilities with respect to safeguarding as well as obligations to support the young person. Reflecting on a relationship with one mother, a senior practitioner (LA 12) stated:

> 'I saw some stuff that was not good and I had to report her. ... [O]ur relationship after that went, that was the end of it really, she didn't want to engage at all after that, and I had known her for [many years], I had a great relationship with her, but I saw some stuff that was concerning and it was game over then. ... [I]t was horrible for her I'm sure, but it was horrible for me that this relationship had gone.'

Similarly, examples of practice dilemmas and/or the potential for compromised relationships with young people included a variety of situations:

> '[W]e do have occasions when people run out of food or run out of electricity and, you know, and that is problematic because not only are they not meeting their own and their child's needs but they know that by coming to us ... coming to us and asking us for help in that situation, would trigger us to think about are there other things to be looking into?' (Team manager LA 8)

> '[W]hen you have those situations it's quite difficult then for the young person to accept that we do have to share concerns, we do have to, you know, take on board those risk factors. ... [W]e have had cases, unfortunately, where young people have said that actually they're going to disengage with us because they don't want us to share information and that's something we know we have to say, really honestly, "Well we can't work with you in that way, you know we can't have a confidentiality to you where

> there's risks involved, we have to share that information.'" (Team manager LA 19)

> 'Ultimately you are a social worker and you are part of the local authority and you can't get away from that so actually if you go out and you see a concern in that household, you need to do something about it.' (Team manager LA 13)

These comments emphasise professional dilemmas and challenges in managing responsibilities with respect to safeguarding, with those of supporting parents in and leaving care. On the one hand, professionals may be key sources of support for young people, the individuals young people turn to in times of difficulty. Yet, on the other hand, professionals have obligations to the state or local authority, including remaining alert to risk and working alongside, as well as sharing information with, other professionals. The tension inherent in these dual roles has the potential to thwart or compromise relationships with young people. As described in the next example, child protection concerns are prioritised and leaving-care professionals can be expected to play a full and active role in the assessment process.

> 'So I made what's called a multi-agency referral and that goes to an intake team who then do assessments. So bearing in mind they do those assessments but they also want information off me and all my visits and anything I pick up is fed in and that's, in this case it was negative. It was very much this mother can't care for her child, she will not be keeping her child, so they did the child protection stuff before the baby was born and the decision was the baby would be removed at birth. So my role had to change then and actually I was there for the removal to be there to support the mum as her social worker and it's a rocky road, you know it is a dual responsibility on the one hand, but once that baby is gone your role then is the mother, to make sure she is a looked after child still, she is under 18.' (Team manager LA 4)

Notwithstanding the importance of safeguarding responsibilities, it is also important to note that the dual responsibilities of professionals do not typically mirror tensions or relationships in families. While in a small minority of cases birth parents may feel the need to officially report concerns regarding child welfare, it is more likely that parents would offer as much financial, emotional and/or practical support as necessary or possible. It is also unlikely that loyalties to children and young parents would be segregated, but rather considered in terms of a family unit. In contrast, the comments of professionals suggest that, for young people in and leaving care, support from key corporate parenting figures is conditional, partial or at risk of disruption.

Discussion: systemic disadvantage and limited corporate parenting protection

Previous chapters have presented evidence of poorer outcomes for parents in and leaving care, and queried the propensity for such findings in light of multiple professional involvement and resources. The findings of this chapter provide valuable insights in furthering efforts to understand such outcomes, and suggest that parents in and leaving care face pervasive stigma and multi-level disadvantage. From the outset, professional confidence in young people's parenting capacity is undermined because of the potential impact and influence of past experiences. Important to note was the lack of confidence with which professionals discussed the ability of the system to undo, repair or compensate for previous experiences of poor or abusive parenting. This is a damning indictment of the system designed to care for the most vulnerable children and young people. Particularly unsettling is the suggestion that experiences in care may compound rather than compensate for young people's lack of exposure to 'good' or 'normal' parenting.

The interviews also highlighted the potential for parents to be treated differently based on their care status. While differences were observed in how professionals and teams typically responded to pregnant and parenting young people; encompassing explicit and implicit expectations to routinely refer young people for parenting assessment, as well as directives to consider individual circumstances, rather than care status, the findings nevertheless demonstrated an increased likelihood of statutory referral and assessment. In addition to the potential for leaving-care professionals to raise concerns about the influence of past experiences, the interviews also suggested endemic stigma across the wider network of professionals. Moreover, structural disadvantage and discrimination means that parents in and leaving care are not only more likely to be subject to statutory referral and assessment but also to extensive historical scrutiny. While the importance of child protection efforts should not be downplayed, such practices nevertheless highlight a marked disparity in responses and treatment for care-experienced parents, in comparison to non-care-experienced young parents.

The findings of this chapter are consistent with themes identified in previous research, with parents both seen and treated differently because of their care status. Connolly et al's (2012) synthesis of qualitative research published between 2001 and 2010 highlighted the potential for parents in and leaving care to be stigmatised and labelled 'at risk', and the findings do little to counter previous assertions of a 'presumed incompetency' (Mantovani and Thomas 2014) or expectations of intergenerational care experience (Rutman et al 2002; Haight et al 2009).

More positively, and also noted in previous research, the findings highlight the potential for leaving-care professionals to be a valuable source of support to parents (Chase et al 2009), able to advocate on their behalf and provide important counter-narratives which emphasise resilience rather than risk. Nevertheless, the findings suggest such efforts may be futile, overpowered by the prioritisation of safeguarding efforts and curtailed by notions of dual responsibilities and divided loyalties (Rutman et al 2002).

Conclusion

In conclusion, the reflections of professionals in this chapter raise concerns about the ability of the current system to adequately prepare young people for parenthood, to protect them from stigma and discrimination as parents, and ensure consistent corporate parenting support. Viewed in this way, there is an urgent need to consider the foundations afforded to children and young people to encourage future parenting 'success', to incorporate safeguards to ward off discrimination based on care status, as well as to ensure young people remain protected and prioritised by all with corporate parenting responsibilities.

The findings of this chapter provide an important basis from which to consider the perspectives of parents in and leaving care. The following chapter will explore young people's early journeys as new parents, including the hopes attached to parenthood, as well as the perception of corporate parent support and involvement.

5

The experiences of parents: hopes, anxieties and reflections

Introduction and background

This chapter is dedicated to the perspectives of care-experienced parents. As experts in their own lives, the participation of parents in and leaving care enabled invaluable insights into the experience and impact of parenthood on their lives. The reflections of parents provide further contextual detail to help consider issues of early pregnancy and parenthood (discussed in Chapter 2) as well as risks of state intervention and separation for children born to parents in and leaving care (discussed in Chapters 3 and 4). Parents' reflections provide a helpful source for contrast and comparison with professional perspectives, and offer an important foundational base from which to consider issues of support in the next chapter.

Previous research has highlighted the potential for early pregnancy and parenthood to be viewed as a positive aspiration and choice by young people in and leaving care. For example, Biehal and Wade (1996) noted positive connotations related to parenting identity and suggested that becoming a parent offered a sense of belonging, stability and hope for the future. Similar claims were made by Haydon (2003), who noted the potential for parenthood to provide a socially acceptable role. Accordingly, pregnancy and parenthood may be considered 'a force for good' (Mantovani and Thomas, 2014), and be a source of motivation or 'turning point' for positive change (Barn and Mantovani 2007; Haight et al 2009). Aparicio (2015) noted that parents were motivated to keep children out of the care system and to parent differently – better than they had been. Similarly, parents in Rolfe's (2008) study reflected on the need to grow up and accept responsibility in their efforts to 'do things differently' for their children.

Despite such hopes, parenthood has been noted to bring hardship and challenges. In Corylon and McGuire's (1999) research, pregnancy and parenthood were seen as a powerful motivator for change, but parenting was hampered by a lack of information, role models, and informal and formal supports. More recently, Pryce and Samuels (2010) found that attempts to be good and better parents were inhibited by poverty and lack of support.

Participants in Maxwell et al's study (2011) reflected on the ideal versus the realities of motherhood, experiencing it as rewarding but also overwhelming, and feeling the need for support while also perceiving it as intrusive and invasive. This corresponds with the work of Haight et al (2009: 58), who noted that mothers faced multiple stigmas, with respect to care experience, race and age, and described professionals as overly critical of their parenting abilities. Providing a rare focus on the perspectives of fathers, Tyrer et al (2005) highlighted exclusion as a recurring theme, including exclusion from decision making, relationships, contact and services designed to support parenting. As noted in Chapter 4, care-experienced parents can be reluctant to seek support, fearing unhelpful interference and monitoring by social workers (Corylon and McGuire 1999; Chase et al 2009; Mantovani and Thomas 2014).

Despite adversity, parenthood has been described as positive and stabilising (Connolly et al 2012). Chase et al (2006: 442) observed that parents in their study frequently reported children as having a calming and positive impact on their lives; crediting children with having 'turned their lives around'. Wade (2008) also found that parents were largely positive about their new family lives and reflected warmly on being needed and having a sense of purpose. Motherhood has the potential to be a positive and repairing experience for care-experienced women (Maxwell et al 2011), while for fathers it has the potential to bring to an end destructive behaviours and assist efforts to accept responsibility (Reeves 2006). Related to this, Creswell (2019) noted the 'symbolic' value of parenting for young people and its role in helping to forge a 'post-care identity'.

Findings from the Voices study

Participating parents were predominantly recruited through third-sector organisations in Wales. While some participated for a single interview, others agreed to a follow-up interview approximately one year later. This chapter combines the data generated from these interviews, and charts experiences and reflections of parents from the discovery of pregnancy, through the initial months and years of children's lives. The chapter includes the perspectives of parents who, despite periods of significant adversity, were successfully caring for their children, as well as those separated from their children, and who had minimal influence and input in their children's lives.

Becoming a parent

Initial shock and early commitment

Each of the parents reflected on their initial reactions about the prospect of parenthood. The vast majority described being surprised or shocked on discovery of the pregnancy:

> 'When she told me she was pregnant I didn't believe her so I went and bought like five more boxes of pregnancy tests and all of them came up positive and I don't know, I just went missing for like a week no one heard from me in like a week. … I came back after like a week and I just said to her that I'd go with whatever she decided.' (Shane)

> 'Yeah I was shocked, I cried. I wasn't happy at all. … I absolutely pooed myself, I'm not going to lie.' (Charlotte)

> 'I was shocked. I hadn't been trying to get pregnant. It was just one of those things.' (Eve)

> 'It just happened, I didn't really think I'd get pregnant because me and my partner of five years we'd been having unprotected sex for ages and it's just something we never thought of and then I ended being pregnant then three years into the relationship and just went from there then really.' (Kim)

Few participants recalled being supported to access contraception and the majority stated they were not actively seeking to prevent pregnancy. Despite some professional confidence in the potential of the system to identify and respond to young people's sexual health needs (discussed in Chapter 2), the reflections of parents failed to corroborate that there was a coordinated or tailored system responding to needs, or an abundance of opportunities to access support. Rather, the findings resonate with previous suggestions that young people can have a 'fatalistic acceptance' (Corylon and McGuire 1999) of the future rather than feeling they have agency over the trajectories of their lives. The exception to this was Sadie, who stated she had been actively trying to get pregnant. At 15, the prospect of having a baby seemed to provide an escape from difficult childhood experiences and offered the promise of a stable, loving family relationship: "I just thought something that was mine and because I never had the family unit ... I just slept around trying to get caught by anyone." Sadie's comments highlight the emotional influences on early pregnancy and are consistent with the perspectives of social care professionals (Chapter 2) who argued that ensuring access to contraception was insufficient in isolation.

Despite some initial surprise, several participants discussed being quickly committed to becoming parents and were opposed to the possibility of terminating the pregnancy:

> 'I was pregnant and I sat there and I cried and cried and cried and cried. But I wouldn't get rid of her because I knew, like I am against abortions, I think everybody has them for their own reasons but sometimes they're just not good enough, do you know what I mean? But and I feel like every child deserves a chance to at least have a life like give it up for adoption or something and I couldn't ... I couldn't get rid of her.' (Rebecca)

> 'Because when I had my scan it was a baby, he was a very big baby as well so I couldn't really go through getting an abortion with him, it would be killing another little human.' (Nic)

> 'No, I didn't even have that conversation. I just don't like that sort of thing if that makes sense.' (Aaron)

The parents' comments are consistent with previous research findings that care-experienced young people as more likely to continue a pregnancy to live birth (Craine et al 2014). Despite sometimes recognising the timing and circumstances were not ideal to have a baby, participants in this study often spoke with pride at the decision to continue with the pregnancy. These comments may reflect young people's moral beliefs, a willingness to accept responsibility for the consequences of their actions, and/or a positive inclination towards becoming a parent. Despite initial feelings of shock, some young people were pleased at the prospect of having a baby and viewed the pregnancy with optimism and hope for the future:

> '[I thought] wow I'm pregnant, I've got a baby. I've got someone to like play with, look after. Someone that makes me smile and laugh with them.' (Sophie)

> 'I knew I was going to keep the baby. ... I'm excited now but scared at the same time. It's going to be my baby. I've always wanted one. I'm having a boy. Since I was 16 I've wanted one, but then at the start of the year I stopped wanting one but I ended up having one. I don't know why, I've just always wanted one. I just want to be with the baby and give it love, love that I never had really.' (Sam)

Sam's and Sophie's comments resonate with the perspectives of professionals in Chapter 2, which suggested that young people can be attracted to early parenthood because of the associated emotional bonds and familial connections. Previous literature has also suggested that parenthood offers a valued social role, provides a sense of purpose and can be perceived as having the potential to offer emotional fulfilment (Haydon 2003; Connolly et al 2012).

Wanting to be better and do better

Parents' care experiences were frequently referenced during the interviews, and several parents discussed feeling failed, unwanted, abandoned or rejected by parents. Common across interviews when discussing the prospect of becoming parents was a discernible wish to do better and be better parents for their children. Similar findings were noted by Weston (2013), who discussed parents' strong desire to be 'good parents' but were often simultaneously fearful of 'the cycle repeating'. Parents in this study often made reference to their own childhood as a way of highlighting what they did not want their children to experience.

> 'I just don't want the kid being taken away. [I want the baby's childhood to be a] good one yeah, different to what I had. No fighting, no robbing, no like involvement with drugs and stuff like that. ... Like just more chilled out like because my parents were always arguing and fighting and shit like that.' (Aaron)

> 'Like the way that I have been brought up like I wouldn't want my daughter to ever have that kind of lifestyle. And like I've always said, whenever I did have kids I'm going to make sure that they have a better life than I did. ... I don't want my daughter having like the life that I have had, like not seeing her dad and stuff. ... Like before my daughter was born like I bought everything for her like way before

she was born. Like they [social workers] can never say that she ever needed for anything.' (Shane)

Aaron's reflections emphasised the importance of protecting his child from criminality as well as unhealthy lifestyles and relationships. Shane had little contact with his father throughout his childhood, and made reference to this to highlight the importance of an ongoing relationship with his daughter. In contrast to his experiences of poverty, Shane felt a responsibility to provide for his child and took pride in the interview in detailing the clothes and equipment he had bought for her. This could be related to other examples where parents made reference to their own childhood experiences as a way of explaining their aspirations and goals as parents:

'It's made me not want to be like my parents; I never want my kids to grow up like I grew up, you know I am not having that, there is no chance in hell. My kids are going to want to come home, my kids are going to know that I'm here for them, my kids are going to know right from wrong, you know, my kids are going to know [talks to baby] "Yes you are, you're going to know that mummy and daddy love you, aren't you? I don't care, yes you are."' (Charlotte)

'I want to be a better mum than what my mother was. I want to do everything opposite that my mother ever done because she never got involved with me when I was a child, she never took an interest in what I was doing or anything but, like, I want to be there for Ellie, with all her achievements and ups and downs, I just want to be there for her, I want her to know that I'm always there for her, good and the bad. Her school work, I want to get involved with all that when she goes to school because my mother was never bothered about my schooling or anything like that, she never used to come to any of my plays or anything like that so I want Ellie to know that I am, I will always be there for her like basically so I just want to be a good mother to her.' (Kim)

'I want to make a life for my kids. I might be on benefits now but I'm not going to be on benefits for the rest of my life. I know what I want to do, I set my mind straight and I am going to make my kids proud. That was my main thing, it's like I am not going to sit here and be one of them parents that, you know, they need to be taught that anything is possible and that they can do it. … Yeah, because I don't want her to get, I don't want her to think that, you know, I am horrible and all I do is shout. You know, I want my daughter to love me and respect me.' (Rebecca)

The comments show a strong desire among participants to be better and do better for their children, with previous experiences providing a reference for what to avoid in parenting. Yet while the wish to be better parents was evident in the vast majority of the interviews, in some examples, past experiences had the potential to undermine young people's confidence in their parenting ability:

'I'm sat there thinking, doubting myself: I don't want to be like my mum, I don't want this to happen to my child, I don't want her to go [into care], I don't want her to go like somewhere where she doesn't know, do you know what I mean? I want her to live with me, I want to do what I never had.' (Bethany)

'I had a lot of worries when I was pregnant because of my childhood; there was a lot of serious things that had gone on in my childhood that had sort of messed with my mind in a way, if you like. … I didn't feel confident about becoming a mum, because I didn't have no knowledge of being a parent and what a parent was. … I'd had the physical skills there … but I didn't have the … the emotional knowledge and support there and the confidence in myself to become the sole parent of a baby sort of thing, it was quite a huge thing.' (Amy)

These comments highlight potential consequences of stigma (Goffman 1963), with some parents also questioning the impact of the past and doubting their ability to be different and do things differently for their children. The potential to see parenting ability as inhibited or damaged by previous experiences has previously been noted in the perspectives of professionals (Chapter 4). However, it is important to acknowledge that parents repeatedly made explicit their wish to be 'good' parents and to ensure more positive childhood experiences for their children. Rather than normalising or being at risk of replicating childhood experiences, young people frequently made reference to aspects of their care as unacceptable and not good enough for their child. The comments are not intended to suggest that parents necessarily knew how to be 'good' parents; several of the parents quoted here experienced a range of difficulties that would inhibit parenting. However, overall the section's findings highlight parents' strong motivation to be successful parents and to avoid intergenerational experiences of care.

Fear and mistrust of social workers

Connected to issues of the past and individuals' hopes and fears about parenting, repeated references were made regarding the possibility of social work involvement and intervention. Such anxieties had the potential to weigh heavily on young people and impact on their experiences before and after giving birth. For example, on discovering she was pregnant Kim stated: "the first thing that came into my mind was social services". Similarly Anna stated: "the first question I asked my leaving-care worker was 'Are you going to make a referral?'". Leah stated she was anxious "throughout my pregnancy because social got involved, I was really scared", while Molly reflected: "It was always in my mind because I had social services most of my life and I didn't want him to have them."

In addition to fears of intrusion, parents also noted examples of direct contact. For example, Carly stated she had received a phone call from social workers "asking questions". Having answered the questions, Carly was informed that further enquiries would be made with connected professionals, and providing no concerns were raised, the case would be closed. Despite hearing nothing further in the proceeding weeks, the uncertainty as to whether social workers were going to "do anything" was a constant source of anxiety in the final stages of her pregnancy: "I just don't know if they are going to turn up when I have the baby or whether that's it." Similar concerns about whether to trust or believe what social workers were saying, were also apparent:

> 'I have had like worries over like social services obviously, I'm like thinking of them taking the baby off me. But I have been told that's not going to happen unless you do something wrong ... but then you don't know ... social services, you know what they're like.' (Bethany)

In her follow-up interview, Bethany reflected on how worries about whether social workers were going to remove her child, impacted on her initial feelings after giving birth by caesarean section:

'I was awake but my head was going ten to a dozen because like I didn't know what was happening, they took her off me and I thought oh what if social are here and they're going to take her off me. That's how I felt, how I thought.'

Bethany's concerns proved to be unfounded; social workers did not attend the hospital and took no further action regarding her child. Nevertheless, her comments highlight the potential for parents to live in constant fear of social work involvement, and the perceived threat of intervention can loom ominously over the pregnancy and birth. Such responses suggest a clear difference in experience for young people in and leaving care: the prospect of anticipated and expected statutory involvement. These comments can be related to the potential for routine referral and assessment of care-experienced parents, discussed in the Chapter 4. While such practices may be well intentioned in terms of proactively identifying needs and investigating risk, such practices also need to be considered from the perspective of young people and in the context of their experiences and histories. There is potential to both induce anxiety and increase stress; reactions which have the potential to cause harm rather than protect or support children.

Not all parents were explicitly critical of their interactions with individual social workers. However, in the majority of interviews, parents expressed frustration at their treatment and reported feeling stigmatised and/or unfairly treated because of their care status:

'If I wasn't a care leaver I think they [social workers] would have just left me alone. Because I made the comment to them, "just because my mum did to me what she did to me, doesn't mean to say I'm going to do that to her". They said "yeah but it has been known". I said "it has been known", I said "but I'm not that person"'. (Charlotte)

'With my first son there were social workers knowing everything [about care history] but they kind of used it against me because they see it as, well if your birth parents did this with you, you're most likely to do it as well and obviously that wasn't the case. It hasn't affected how I am as a parent, it's affected like – I think that's why social services got involved was because I had been in care so they see it as, you know, down the generations it's going to happen again and again and again and again and again.' (Leah)

> 'Once they [social services] found out I'd been in care that was it, they went back pulled up all the files, read them all [and] seen what had happened ... they read those records some of which had been written ten years previously. They judged me and used it against me.' (Sarah)

> 'We [James and his partner] were both in care for similar reasons. Violence was a massive part of it, that's what's made them [social workers] a bit nervous, the fact that whether or not we would treat him [their son] the same way. I said in court, I said, realistically, if you look at it from our point of view, we're not going to do that, now we've been through it ourselves, we're going to want to give him a better life compared to what we had.' (James)

The accounts highlight a paradox in parents aspiring to do better and be better for their children, while conscious that views and assessments of them are heavily influenced by the past. The quotations resonate with Critchley's (2019b) study of pre-birth child protection. The comments similarly suggest parents 'struggling to be heard' but also chime with Critchley's (2019a) notions of defeatism and resistance. While some parents appeared resigned to involvement of social workers, a sense of injustice was more frequently apparent. Parents in this study typically rejected assumptions that they posed risks to their children and, rather, conceived the risks as emanating from the state.

> 'They [Children's Services] wanted to take her from birth. The social worker said to me "there's not many that break the cycle". She said that to me! ... They had a child protection conference when I was 35 weeks pregnant. I was so stressed and didn't know what was going to happen. Thank God, the IRO [Independent Reviewing Officer or Conference Chair] was really good. She said "all these risks are historical, there's nothing current". She told them "everyone needs to calm down, the stress is going to put this girl into early labour."' (Anna)

The quote from Anna similarly highlights the potential for professional resistance (Critchley 2019a) whereby the IRO rejected deterministic perceptions of parenting capacity based on historical concerns. Yet, as discussed in Chapter 4, young people's past experiences have the potential to taint professionals' views of parents and historical records have the potential to further contribute to disadvantage. While the propensity for social workers to consider the influence of past experiences chimes with popular theoretical frameworks such as Attachment Theory (Bowlby 1969; Ainsworth et al 1978; Hazan and Shaver 1987), the comments from parents emphasise the potential for this to be stigmatising and oppressive, with the likely consequence of increasing stress and anxiety. In contrast, parents' comments can be related to concepts of resilience (Stein 2005), where young people were explicit in their desire to avoid past experiences and forge more positive experiences for their children.

While the majority of parents discussed being referred to Children's Services during pregnancy or around the time of birth, some parents also had experiences of subsequent or repeated referrals. For example, Molly had no ongoing contact with social workers at the time of interview, but disclosed her experience of twice being referred to Children's Services because of concerns about her parenting: "So they come out, they check your house, your kid, see if he's got any bruises on him or something stupid like that. And then they're off, basically. ... They come out and they've stayed a couple of weeks and said everything is fine."

Molly expressed some frustration about the nature of the concerns. She stated the reasons given for the concerns were: "leaving my child with other people ... then the other one I think it was because he had old nappies or something, or clothes. But stuff like stupid stuff basically". Reflecting on the experience, she added: "I left [child] with a friend. I had, that one was right. I even admitted it, I said to them I leave him with a friend. But that friend was trusted by me. Who doesn't leave their kids at some point?" Molly's comments are consistent with previous findings, indicating minimal opportunities for support for some parents. Such comments highlight the potential for parents to be doubly disadvantaged; while support available from corporate parents was recognised by professionals as a poor substitute for the support typically available within birth families (see Chapter 4), young people can nevertheless be criticised for drawing on their limited resources. Noteworthy from Molly's account is the suggestion that social workers would investigate and monitor the situation to ensure there were no safeguarding concerns and then leave. This can be related to recent critiques of social work practice which suggest an 'investigative turn' (Bilson et al 2017) that is adept at highlighting parenting inadequacies but fails to provide the necessary supports to help families overcome difficulties (Featherstone et al 2014). The experiences noted earlier similarly stand in contrast to

Gupta and Blumhardt's (2016) assertion that in child protection contexts, trust in professionals as well as the availability of basic help is important.

In another example, Rebecca discussed an incident where her personal adviser noticed a small bruise on her baby:

> 'I don't know, it was just one of those things, like it was genuinely one of those things. But the thing is like the worker, she seen it and then reported it and took me down the doctor's. In all fairness though to her, she did take me to the doctor's, she took me. She asked me to ring social services myself and I was like: "I can't, don't ask me to ring social services on myself, you know I already get enough hassle as it is, don't make me do that." So I was like: "You can do it and you can do it right in front of me, but I will not be speaking to them."'

Rebecca's reflections illuminate the dual responsibilities of leaving-care professionals to act on potential safeguarding concerns, as well as support young people. While Rebecca appreciated the worker's open communication and supportive attempts to address the situation together, the frustration and exasperation at the forced referral was clearly apparent. As in the example of Molly earlier, this young mother's understandings of social work involvement were presented unfavourably, constructed as adding to difficulties, as opposed to being a potential source of support.

Molly's and Rebecca's experiences are indicative of generally poor reflections on relationships and interactions with assessing social workers. There was a tendency to discuss social work intervention as procedural, investigatory and unhelpful. Rather than being presented as individuals who could provide help and support, or as individuals with corporate parenting responsibilities, social workers were frequently discussed in negative terms. This included being viewed with fear and suspicion or being regarded as adversaries. Caution was repeatedly expressed as to the extent to which social workers were perceived as wanting parents to succeed, their ability to provide meaningful help and the extent to which they could be trusted. For example, Anna stated: "I can't trust them, they don't do what they say they are going to do, they don't stick to anything, everything is done behind your back. You can never trust them."

Some parents undergoing current assessment or monitoring were reluctant to discuss their experiences. One couple did not want the interview to be audio recorded for fear that their comments would be heard by social workers and used against them. The couple believed social workers, as well as other connected professionals, were "wanting us to fail" and "are not on our side" (Matt and Tina). Similarly, Sophie declined to discuss her relationship with her social worker and other professionals, simply stating she was complying with "everything that they've asked me to do" in the hope "they won't be long off my back".

As noted in Chapter 4, obligations to protect children are of primary importance in social work and the tensions within practice with respect to care and control are well rehearsed (Dominelli 2009). Similarly, Gibson (2019) recently pointed to issues of shame and shaming for parents subject to child protection procedures. Viewed in this way, the perspectives of parents may, in part at least, be reflective of the nature and purpose of the social work intervention. However, the perspectives of parents in this study arguably do require further consideration as the professionals young people fear, mistrust and view as unhelpful are part of their corporate parenting family, on whom they can be heavily reliant.

Reflecting on parenthood

Struggle and 'success'

While interviews with parents typically suggested an omnipresent concern about potential or actual social work intervention, parents also reflected more broadly about being parents and the ways in which parenthood had impacted on their lives. For those who remained primary carers for their children, parenthood had the potential to have a transformative effect:

> 'I look at them [children] as being my life fixers really because they've done such a big thing for me, the best thing I can give them is a good life now. … I don't see myself as being that person any more, I feel like a new person now.' (Amy)

In other examples, parents recognised challenges as well as rewards associated with parenting. These included struggling without sleep, managing challenging behaviours and dealing with partner or wider family issues. Notwithstanding the challenges presented by some of these issues, parents' reflections remained primarily positive:

'Living with his temper at the moment is really hard [laughs]. But then the good parts is just watching him learn and grow, it's amazing. It's the best experience I've ever had. You do have negatives and all that but I love it, I wouldn't change it for the world. Yeah it has, it's made my life better.' (Molly)

'The health visitor says she's very advanced for her age, she's done everything before she was one. She's eating by herself with her spoon, she's running around, yeah the health visitor says she's thriving really. So yeah in terms of [baby] I'm not finding anything difficult with her apart from her sleeping, otherwise she's great through the day. She is so loving, she's … oh she's great.' (Kim)

'I do enjoy it like you know, we have his [partner's] other child on the weekend … so it's nice. They can be a handful I'm not going to lie, they can, I'm not going to sit here and say it's easy, no they can be a right handful. You know his older one is up the stairs going like "Oh I hate you", you know and hitting his brother and stuff like that so you know they can be a right handful. But it's the joys of being parents.' (Leah)

The challenges and rewards of parenting described by these mothers are likely to resonate with many other parents. As has been noted in previous literature (Chase et al 2006; Wade 2008), despite challenges, parents generally reflected positively on the impact of parenthood on their lives. For parents who retained care of their children, they repeatedly spoke with pride about their children, felt they were realising aims to be better and do better, and enjoyed the emotional connections associated with parenting and family life. However, as noted in Weston's (2013) research, parenthood can be both a challenging as well as a rewarding experience for care-experienced young people. In this study, the reflections of one young person, Rebecca, somewhat differed from the positive reflections just quoted and suggested she was finding the experience particularly difficult.

'[Parenting is] hard. It's the fact that you're constantly having a fight. … [I]t's the best feeling but it's hard and nobody can be like "It's easy, you know I don't struggle", you know. I find it bloody hard [laughs]. I struggle, of course

> I struggle … you know it is the best feeling but sometimes of course you're going to want to slam your head against the wall [laughs] … because everybody is always "I love being a mother, my kids are this, my kids are that" and it's always the good things everybody else says, you never have the mother going "It's noisy, it's hard, I don't want to do this anymore."' (Rebecca)

During her initial interview Rebecca had two young children and was living with her partner. At her follow-up interview, her relationship had ended, she was living as a single parent, housed in an unfamiliar area and was expecting another child with a new partner. With limited access to support and with pregnancy-related health issues, the pressures of caring for two young children had significantly increased:

> 'I wouldn't change them for the world. Being a mother is everything to me, you know, it is. I could not imagine not having my kids. It is just very hard at the minute. You know I sit there like, don't get me wrong … when they're going at it and I have to sit there and I'll be like right, remember why you are doing this. … [T]here has been [times] where I have literally just been "I don't want to do this anymore … you know I can't do this anymore, I don't want to do this anymore." But then you get to that last little point of like "I really can't do it", and then you remember the whole reason why you wanted to do it. … I hate being a mother but I love being a mother.'

As a case example, Rebecca's situation could arguably constitute parenting 'success'; she was living independently, was adding to her family and had no ongoing social work involvement. However, Rebecca's comments suggest she is regularly struggling to cope; she positions herself as different from other parents and there are times where she questions her ability and motivation to continue. While such emotions may resonate with many parents, it is necessary to consider who parents in and leaving care have to call on in such circumstances. For individuals like Rebecca, there may be few opportunities available for support. This disadvantaged position is compounded by corporate parenting support being limited to office hours, which may initiate further referrals to Children's Services, that are understood as adding to, rather than easing difficulties.

Continuing struggle and perceived failure

This section focuses on the perspectives of parents who experienced the removal of one or more children from their care. As noted in other areas of this book, it is not the intention of this study to analyse the decisions or pass judgement on the trajectories of individual parents and children. It is acknowledged that the reflections of parents may stand in contrast to those of other connected parties. However, these comments are important in understanding the perspectives of parents and thinking through continuing support needs.

For parents who had experienced the removal of a child, ongoing struggle and unhappiness was evident. Feelings of anger and resentment often dominated parents' narratives and an enduring sense of injustice was apparent:

> 'When the social workers were involved like they were saying to us, they were just here to help you, give some support, just to give you some advice, point me in the right directions. ... The day he was born, not before, not once, but from the day one they said that they don't think that we would be able to handle [child's name], they don't think we had the right parenting skills to be able to look after him.' (James)

> 'They came and saw me when I was three months pregnant and it was like "Yeah, everything is fine, no concerns." Then the day she is born everybody is in court.' (Emma)

> 'I used to tell her [the social worker] I hate her. ... Basically they [social services] never wanted [child's name] to come back [and be placed in Tara's care], that's why they left me to it.' (Tara)

> 'They reckoned I couldn't cope. I did everything they asked, he was always fed, washed, dressed. I was doing it.' (Eve)

> 'Even most of the judges who dealt with my kids' cases have said to social services, "It is your fault she is the way she is, if you brought her up correctly she would know how to sustain a lifestyle to enable her to look after her children."' (Sadie)

Parents' sense of injustice over previous events and their inability to retain care of their children was a source of enduring emotional distress, and they were often keen to make clear that separation from their children was not something that they wanted or had chosen:

> 'They [social services] made out I was scum. They tried to say I didn't love her. … I didn't want her to be adopted. I didn't want her to go into foster care. All I wanted was some help and support.' (Sarah)

> 'The way they [social services] wrote it up was that I gave her up, that I didn't want her. But I did want her. I still do want her.' (Emma)

Such accounts resonate with Morriss' (2018) notion of haunted motherhood, with mothers feeling silenced, stigmatised and shamed. Yet while a sense of injustice was common within parents' reflections, so too were feelings of personal regret, self-blame and internalised messages of failure:

> 'It feels horrible because I know there's things I could've done differently. … But I was a child myself, I needed help and support and I wasn't getting it.' (Leanne)

> 'I felt so much guilt, so much shame in the fact that I let her [partner] down, let myself down, worst of all I felt like I let [son's name] down and the fact that I failed as a parent and that's one thing I always said, I didn't want any of this to happen to him.' (James)

> 'It's like on Mother's Day, people say "Oh you're a mother" but no I'm not.' (Emma)

Parents described few opportunities for support and comfort following the loss of a child. In some instances, the loss had initiated further difficulties within participants' lives:

> 'The day they took the baby off me, I collapsed on the floor. I cried and I cried and I cried. It's made me have mental health problems. It's affected the rest of my life.' (Emma)

'I did turn to drink, I did start doing drugs, I won't deny that, I'm not proud of it but when you've experienced something like that you just turn to anything that kind of helps to forget those kind of memories. ... I'm not the person who I used to be, you know, I suffer with depression a lot now. I've attempted suicide ... the entire process has had a massive impact on my life and it probably will now for the rest of it.' (James)

'Like I went downhill, I hit alcohol, drugs. ... I went totally mad, I had no support off no one.' (Tara)

'I don't speak to anyone, I just can't go out and face it.' (Eve)

As well as deteriorations in mental health and increased destructive behaviour, some parents experienced the withdrawal of housing and financial support, while others reported returning to unhealthy relationships as a means of comfort or support. For example, Sadie had attempted to end her violent relationship but stated:

'They were going to take [child's name] anyway and [partner's name] was at the hospital, he was there when I was breaking my heart, he was the one hugging me when they took him so I fell back for him. And then three months later, I was pregnant again.'

Sadie's subsequent child was similarly removed from her care as there had been insufficient opportunity for her to demonstrate positive change.

The comments here relate to previous discussions, where parents were critical of their relationships and interaction with social workers. Collectively, the comments allege inadequate support, together with an absence of open communication and clarity with respect to parenting expectations. In addition, parents may also apportion blame to themselves, wrestling with regret and burdened by failures to be better and do better for their children. While the support needs of parents who have experienced the removal of a child have recently gained attention (Neil 2006; Broadhurst and Mason 2017; Fidler 2018; Hinton 2018; Morriss 2018) and resulted in the development of valuable support services (Lewis-Brooke et al 2017; McCracken et al 2017; Roberts et al 2018), parents in the Voices study were typically offered minimal support in reconciling past events or in attempts to move towards more positive futures. Rather, parents were left to manage their feelings and situations, often with limited supportive options and vulnerable to destructive influences and behaviours. Instead of young people perceiving corporate parents as individuals to whom they can turn for support, statutory figures are often depicted as central to young people's difficulties but absent in efforts to provide recourse and repair.

Discussion: enduring stigma, and the residual threat of social work intervention

This chapter was intended to offer insight into young people's perspectives; to detail their hopes, anxieties and reflections with regard to becoming and being parents. It is important to note that the young people that participated in the research had varied histories, experiences and outcomes as parents. The heterogeneity of care-experienced parents foregrounds the challenges explored in the next chapter regarding potential efforts to improve policy and practice support for this group.

The findings discussed in this chapter highlight areas of both commonality and difference in parenting. Some of the reflections will likely resonate with parents beyond those who are young or care experienced. For example, feelings of initial shock and surprise, adjusting to the prospect of parenthood and experiencing parenting as both challenging and rewarding, will likely have broad applicability. Similarly, recent critiques of social work as authoritarian and procedural, adept at highlighting parenting inadequacies but ineffectual in providing the necessary supports to help families overcome difficulties (Featherstone et al 2014), extend beyond practice with care-experienced parents. In addition, the emotional trauma associated with enforced separation from a child is not unique to parents in and leaving care (Broadhurst and Mason 2013).

Despite these overlaps, the findings presented in this chapter also suggest that young people's experiences as parents are influenced by their care status. Most striking was the consistency with which parents reported their eagerness to avoid intergenerational patterns of care experience and to ensure more positive childhood experiences for their children. Yet such motivations were typically juxtaposed with ever present anxieties about social work involvement. Assessment and intervention for care-experienced parents is portrayed as routine; resented by some, normalised and tolerated by others. Moreover, young people perceive professionals' knowledge and access to historical information as consolidating risk and compounding stigma.

Such findings resonate with previous literature and there is a notable consistency in accounts from young people across different contexts and countries. For example, evidence reviews by Svoboda et al (2012) and Connolly et al (2012) found that care-experienced young people can have high hopes for family life and want better parenting experiences for their children, but also highlight difficulties with respect to stigma and a persistent fear of social worker intervention.

Crucially, the reflections of parents in this study provide no indication that corporate parenting responsibilities prompt additional supports or safeguards. For young people who retain care of their children, parenting has the potential to be enriching and transformative, sometimes offering repair and recovery from past events (Barn and Mantovani 2007; Maxwell et al 2011). Yet such examples were typically portrayed as being achieved aside from or in spite of, rather than as a result of corporate parenting support. Similarly, caring for children was not always experienced as a 'happy ever after'; parenting was also depicted as challenging and sometimes presented additional hardship for young people. In this way, conceptualisations of 'success' in parenthood need to extend beyond whether children remain in the care of their parents.

While issues of support will be considered in the next chapter, it is significant that corporate parents were often constructed as part of and contributing to such hardship, as opposed to relieving difficulties. Finally, parents who were separated from their children faced further emotional trauma and, in some cases, were at risk of repeat pregnancy and recurrent losses to the care system. In these examples, professionals were typically assigned blame, and prompted feelings of anger and resentment rather than being constructed as a source of support or comfort.

Conclusion

Young people's trajectories as parents fit with Stein's (2012) notion of care leavers moving on, surviving and struggling. Yet across trajectories, rather than being portrayed as a supportive or resourceful parent, the state is more commonly constructed as interfering, unhelpful and potentially punitive. While issues of support will be further explored in Chapter 6, the findings of both this chapter and Chapter 4 raise important issues about the foundations of the relationship between young people in care and their corporate parents. This includes the ways in which young people are seen and responded to as parents, and the supportive obligations and accountability of the state in ensuring parenting 'success'. The findings provide further contextual detail to aid understanding of poor outcomes for care-experienced parents and suggest there is significant scope to improve the relationship between young people and professionals with corporate parenting responsibilities.

The next chapter considers issues of support in more detail. This includes the reflections of parents on their experiences of support provision, as well as the perspectives of professionals, who discuss individual and local efforts to support young people as parents.

6

Responding to diverse needs: support availability, sustainability and acceptability

Introduction and background

This chapter is concerned with support for parents in and leaving care. This includes consideration of how support needs are understood, how they are responded to, and the extent to which support responses are considered appropriate and effective. The chapter brings together the perspectives of leaving-care professionals, who oversee the support for young people leaving care, with the reflections of parents who have personal experience of needing and receiving support. The chapter provides further context for understanding outcomes for parents in and leaving care, and prompts consideration of the adequacy, sustainability and acceptability of state responses and support.

All parents, regardless of age and care experience, will likely need or benefit from help with parenting. This may include a range of practical, emotional and financial support, predominantly provided by partners, family and friends, but also via professionals and locally available groups and services. As illustrated in models showing a continuum of support (Welsh Government 2017) and tiers of service provision (Social Care Institute for Excellence 2012), professional intervention can encompass a range of involvement; including universally available support, targeted provision to address specific or lower level needs, intensive support services to address multiple and more complex needs, as well as specialist interventions to address severe and acute needs. The level of intervention required is likely to be influenced by both parent and child factors. For example, parental factors such as age and care experience have the potential to impact on both support needs and availability. As argued by Haydon (2003: 9): 'Teenage mothers leaving care experience similar difficulties to those faced by all young mothers (concerning parenting, finding a place to live, childcare, accessing education or work). However, they are less likely to have consistent, positive adult support and more likely to have to move.'

Similarly, Murray and Goddard's (2014) review of the literature suggests that care-experienced parents sometimes need extra support as a result of poor experiences of parenting themselves, institutionalisation and reduced support networks. Such findings are consistent with the perspectives of leaving-care professionals detailed in Chapter 4, who expressed concerns about the impact of young people's experiences prior to and during care. However, the findings from the previous chapter showed parents are often highly motivated to ensure better childhood experiences for their children but can feel stigmatised by professionals, subject to unhelpful statutory processes and/or fearful of intervention. Such a context provides an important foundation from which to consider how support needs are understood, developed, responded to and experienced.

Despite the anticipation of increased needs and diminished resources, relatively little is known about the support available or its effectiveness. While positive evidence exists with respect to a range of parenting interventions, including home visiting programmes (Dalziel and Segal 2012) and supports such as Parent–Child Interaction Therapy (Batzer et al 2018), Mellow Parenting (MacBeth et al 2015), Incredible Years (Gardner et al 2017) and Triple P (Saunders et al 2014), their application and effectiveness with care-experienced parents is unknown. Previous studies with care-experienced parents have highlighted the potential for professional involvement to be understood as supportive and encouraging, as well as overly critical, intrusive and imbued with negative judgements with respect to parenting motivation and ability (see Chapter 5; Corylon and Maguire 1999; Haydon 2003; Chase et al 2009; Haight et al 2009; Maxwell et al 2011; Cresswell 2019). In a systematic review of practitioner and foster carer perceptions of the needs of parents in and leaving care, Gill et al (2020) reported a range of challenges connected to parenting whilst in or leaving state care including 'placement issues ... limited resources, role confusion, and insufficient professional development in relation to their work'. With regard to support approaches, the relevance of Attachment Theory and strengths-based approaches, child development knowledge, trauma-informed and social support have been suggested (Scwartz et al 2004; Rothenberg 2005; Budd et al 2006; Muzik et al 2013; Bernard 2015). Stockman and Budd's (1997) survey of 28 support providers in Illinois found that informal modelling and feedback, peer support groups, home visitation and mentoring were considered the most effective parenting interventions for parents with a history of state care. However, the interventions perceived to be most helpful did not necessarily correspond to the interventions used most frequently, and the perspectives of professionals were not supported by objective evidence or the views of care-experienced parents. While reviews of the literature have emphasised the need for holistic approaches, incorporating support with housing, finances, mental and physical health, and social support (Mendes 2009; Connolly et al 2012; Svoboda et al 2012) there remains little evidence in relation to effective interventions (Mullins Geiger and Schelbe 2014; Finnigan-Carr et al 2015; Fallon and Broadhurst 2015). For Finnigan-Carr et al (2015), the lack of evidence has hampered efforts to develop a model of good practice and create parity of provision for care-experienced parents. Moreover, Lieberman et al (2014) have argued that the development of an evidence base is hindered by issues of model fidelity, as well as challenges with conducting and securing support for research.

In accordance with the underdeveloped evidence base, the Voices study sought to explore the range of support available to parents in and leaving care. This included the nature and type of support available, the extent to which support availability is consistent with needs, together with professional and parental reflections on the support available.

Findings from the Voices study

This chapter draws on interview data from both leaving-care professionals and care-experienced parents. The first part of the chapter revisits evidence with respect to identified needs of parents in and leaving care. This includes the range of potential needs that are anticipated by professionals, and the extent to which these correspond with the reflections and personal experiences of parents. The second part of the chapter examines how such support needs are met. This includes professional expectations of parents, access to informal support, as well as the availability and adequacy of professional support and service provision. The findings presented prompt a consideration of the challenges inherent in developing support responses for parents in and leaving care and the extent to which the state as parent can and should seek to replicate the type of support typically provided from grandparents.

The potential for multiple and multifaceted support needs

The survey data presented in Chapter 3 revealed a wide range of support needs for the 259 parents identified over the course of the study. Table 6.1 illustrates the most common needs identified by professionals related to family and relationships, mental health difficulties, housing,

Table 6.1: The number and nature of recorded needs for young people

		Female N	Female %	Male N	Male %	Total N	Total %
Number of recorded needs	0	29	14	7	13	36	14
	1–4 needs	124	60	25	48	149	58
	5+ needs	53	26	20	38	73	28
Recorded needs	Family/relationships	96	15	27	14	123	15
	Mental health	88	14	18	9	106	13
	Housing	79	13	20	10	99	12
	Financial/budgeting	73	12	21	11	94	11
	Education, employment and training	68	11	26	13	94	11
	Domestic abuse	62	10	19	10	81	10
	Independent living skills	59	9	21	11	80	10
	Drugs/alcohol misuse	44	7	23	12	67	8
	Other	27	4	18	9	45	5
	Learning difficulty	14	2	3	2	17	2
	Physical health	11	2	3	2	14	2
	Learning disability	2	0	1	1	3	0
	Total	623	100	200	100	823	100

finances and budgeting, and education, employment and training. While 14 per cent of the sample were recorded as having no support needs, 58 per cent were recorded as having between 1 and 4 needs, and 28 per cent as having 5 or more.

Interviews with professionals highlighted a broad range of support needs. These included needs potentially experienced by any or all parents, such as needing help adapting to being a new parent: "Anybody, whether you have been in care or not, finds it difficult to adjust to being a parent, there are some people who it will come naturally to and some it won't" (Team manager LA 17). For this team manager, the transition to parenthood had the potential to be a challenging experience. This was framed as irrelevant to young people's care experiences, but rather reflective of the demands of parenting. Yet, consistent with the literature (Murray and Goddard 2014) and the findings presented in Chapter 4, practitioners also anticipated additional parenting support needs as a result of a young person's previous experiences:

> 'I think that a lot of our young people have got so many [needs], you know, care histories, so many issues and they can't even begin to properly care for their child, you know, without some sort of intervention.' (Senior practitioner LA 21)

> '[Often] they don't have a lot of the skills … or they haven't developed those skills in a nurturing family. … [T]hey've had very negative experiences of being parented themselves so I think they don't really, they know how they shouldn't be doing it but they don't necessarily know the other way to do it.' (Personal adviser LA 22)

These comments are consistent with the accounts discussed in Chapter 4, where there was a propensity for professionals to suspect that parenting capacity was inhibited or damaged as a result of previous experiences. While recognising the potential for any parent to require support adapting to parenthood, these comments suggest that care-experienced young people would likely require enhanced forms of support. As noted in the comments, there were concerns that parents hadn't had opportunity to develop such skills and wouldn't know how to do it "properly".

In addition to parenting support needs, an array of considerations reflective of parents' individual needs and circumstances, were also highlighted:

> 'I think generally there does seem to be a lot of support needed with finances, links to entitlements. … If they're working, how does that affect it, what would they do about childcare, how would they budget, do they have the skills to manage a tenancy so that obviously includes the budgeting but also includes independent living skills. Self-care skills, you know managing your personal hygiene, doing your clothes shopping. I found recently a lot of young people don't do clothes shopping, their foster carers do it for them, which initially might be fine but, you know, they, and their food shopping, they've never done a food shop. So add that not having those skills with actually having to get those skills suddenly, and also have your parenting skills with a child, which, it is overwhelming having a baby. It's, you know, you've got to have a lot of patience, you've got to manage a lot of things, most of the time while you're

tired and, you know, and so there's a lot to consider.' (Senior practitioner LA 20)

'I think usually financial need, that's a great great need that they have. Housing can be another need. Transport, I mean ... they can be stuck out in the middle of nowhere with nothing you know, so actually even just getting to a midwife appointment causes great difficulty and cost. ... So for a young person that's based here to get up to [hospital] where they go for their midwife appointments it costs £5, when you're on benefits £5 is an awful lot of money you know that's your meal isn't it for one day?' (Team manager LA 9)

'Healthy relationships is a huge one. Budgeting, sort of just role modelling. They can have no idea how to use, like, washing machines and stuff like that. Housing, definitely housing is a huge one. Anger management and the emotional regulation so, to stop them you know going crazy basically. So I think those are the main ones. Oh, employment as well because what it is as well, as you well know, that if they get into a flat they're not going to be able to afford. Drug and alcohol use can be an issue. ... Managing money, manage their emotions, managing tenancy, managing relationships ... managing their social relationships, managing their loneliness as well.' (Senior practitioner LA 4)

These accounts note a comprehensive range of practical, emotional and financial considerations, and are indicative of those across the data, whereby professionals repeatedly framed parenting needs within a myriad of additional needs. Despite the additional needs noted by professionals all being within the supportive remit of the state as parent, the comments suggest the potential for parents to face multiple challenges, with needs directly linked to parenting as well those influenced and exacerbated by experiences prior to, during and while leaving care.

Consistent with interviews with professionals, interviews with parents highlighted a wide range of support needs. For example, managing the demands of parenting was sometimes experienced as isolating, exhausting and overwhelming:

'I'd never been on my own with the baby before, when I was here I mean, I was lonely and I was quite frightened,

I mean I'd never really been in a house on my own before.' (Sophie)

'In all honesty, I need a break. I know that sounds, I know that does sound horrible. It sounds like a really bad thing to come out of a mother's mouth, alright but just a couple of hours.' (Rebecca)

'I didn't have no family to turn to have [baby] to stay overnight so I was having her all the time and she wasn't sleeping very well so I just needed a break, so yeah.' (Kim)

The comments of these mothers highlight needs that may be experienced by any parent; the enormity of responsibility associated with caring for a child and simultaneously being desperate for a break while feeling guilty about needing some time away from parenting. Yet while the needs may be similar, the comments also indicate additional hardship linked to age and care experience. For Sophie, adapting to living alone is intensified with the new responsibility of caring for a baby, and for Kim and Rebecca there is no option of family support to help mitigate feeling overwhelmed with the demands of parenting.

Consistent with the perspectives of professionals, needs identified by parents were not always directly related to parenting. Concerns about accommodation and housing options dominated interviews with some parents. For example, reluctant to accept a place in a hostel because of drug and alcohol use among residents, Nic's anxiety was palpable during her interview: "The baby could be born any minute now really, I've got five days [until due date], so he or she can come whenever and then I'm stuck really with nowhere." Ironically, in seeking to challenge the suitability of the hostel placement and advocating for safe and secure housing for her and her baby, Nic stated she was at risk of being categorised as "intentionally homeless", with ominous consequences in terms of her perceived willingness to work with professionals and her ability to prioritise and provide basic care for her child.

In other examples, parents acknowledged challenges with respect to relationships, with unhealthy or unstable interactions with current or former partners, birth family members and friends. Domestic abuse featured in several parents' accounts, with references ranging from frequent verbal arguments and controlling behaviour, to potentially life-threatening incidents. For example, Bethany discussed threats made by her ex-partner about setting fire to her home while Charlotte recalled being violently attacked while holding her child. In addition, parents reported ex-partners "creating trouble" for them by making false reports to social workers.

Parents also acknowledged personal difficulties as they struggled with the aftermath of traumatic experiences and periods of their lives. For example, Tasha discussed struggling to cope after being sexually abused; her distress over this led to further sexual exploitation and reliance on a range of substances. Similarly, in reference to drug and alcohol misuse, Sadie stated:

> 'Parenting assessment I've always been fine with, I've always been able to change them, feed them, bath them. I did need a little bit of teaching with my oldest but they [social services] said I picked it up quite fast, they were fine with the parenting side of it, it was always my lifestyle.'

Sadie's 'lifestyle' had developed after the death of her parent, the event which triggered her entry into care, and led to her being sexually abused by a carer.

Discussing her mental health difficulties that had originated in childhood, Leanne stated: "I had been asking them [social services] for years for [psychological] help. ... When I had him [her son], I didn't really know how to speak to him. I didn't know how to bond." Leanne's comments correspond with professional concerns discussed in Chapter 4 about parents having the necessary knowledge or opportunity to develop parenting skills. The extent to which Leanne's concerns were reflective of her past experiences, general parenting struggles and anxieties, or the consequences of being stigmatised, is unknown. However, the comments prompt consideration of the position and perspective of parents, including how they may interpret such difficulties, and how they reflect on previous experiences of professional involvement and support. Such experiences and understandings may be influential in terms of perceived readiness or capacity to parent discussed earlier but also in terms of willingness and confidence in professional support responses. These issues will be explored further later in this chapter, but it is important to acknowledge that, while some parents were willing and able to approach professionals for help, others, as noted in Chapter 5, felt stigmatised and were fearful of, rather than receptive to their involvement.

The reflections presented in this section of the chapter demonstrate the potential for parents in and leaving care to experience a spectrum of practical, emotional and financial needs. Some needs are shared with parents generally, while others may be influenced by or reflective of experiences before, during or while leaving state care. Professional reflections highlight potential concerns with respect to young people's capacity or readiness to parent, as well as the ability to provide adequate parenting environments. Support needs can be similarly acknowledged by parents with support needed with respect to fundamentals such as housing, as well as a variety of historical and current personal and relational needs.

The next section is concerned with responses to support needs. This includes the expectations on parents, as well as the availability and adequacy of support.

Parental determination, engagement and responsibility

In contrast to the array of potential needs highlighted for parents in and leaving care, the majority of professionals repeatedly emphasised the importance of individual factors in determining outcomes. This included young people's determination to be parents and their willingness to engage with professionals. It also encompassed the choices made by young people, their level of responsibility and commitment to meeting their child's needs. While recognising that successfully parenting a child was challenging, professionals perceived it to be achievable for young people if they "wanted it enough" and were prepared to do whatever was required. For example, several professionals referred to individual young people who had significantly changed their behaviours as a result of pregnancy. Often described as troubled and troublesome young people, the prospect of being a parent induced a "lightbulb moment" and prompted them to radically change their behaviours. The team manager in (LA 1) stated:

> 'I am thinking particularly of two very challenged young women … who were leading extremely chaotic lives … substance misuse … mental health [problems] … self-harm, suicide attempts, offending, you know that sort of quite high-level behaviour. But literally, as soon as they found out they were pregnant, that was it, everything stopped. Like literally, it was like a switch went off.'

The comments of the team manager emphasise the importance of young people's choices and their ability to individually address problematic or concerning behaviours. Related to this, when discussing a parent who had experienced the permanent and compulsory removal of her child, the social worker (LA 19) attributed the outcome to the young person's priorities and decision making with respect to her partner:

> 'It's sad, really sad in her case because I think we could have tried to get a mother and baby placement together for her, she would have stood a chance of keeping that child but with a partner who … they're quite abusive together in the sense there's a lot of alcohol dependency, a lot of fighting, police called, there was no way, while he was on the scene, she was going to keep that child. So in that case it's really sad because, yes, I think perhaps she might have kept her baby on her own, but she didn't want to be on her own.'

Both accounts suggest that, aside from issues of support and intervention, parents need to demonstrate commitment to positive and responsible lifestyles. Rather than seeing the young people as having as support needs, the comments emphasise individual choice and control. In addition, repeated references were made to the importance of young people being concerned not to replicate previous patterns of family dysfunction. Success was seen as more likely for young people who were aware of shortcomings in the parenting they had experienced and were determined to do better or be better for their children:

> 'When you've got a young person who is really strongly against, not wanting the same experiences that they've had themselves … [who] you can see are going that extra mile because they want to break that cycle. And it's that sort of like, that fierce will, then, to break that cycle and to prove to everyone that I am not like my family, I'm not like mum, I'm not like my dad. That makes it happen for them, I have found that to be really important.' (Senior practitioner LA 13)

The senior practitioner's reference to young people proving themselves to others resonated across the data. In this way, it was seen as important for young people to engage with professionals and be willing to do whatever was asked of them in order to demonstrate their wish to be 'good' parents and their parenting ability. For example, one senior practitioner (LA 20) reflected: "I find that a young person's willingness to engage is a big thing ... if they're willing to engage and willing to take on board advice, willing to try, it helps. When they're saying no, I don't need anything I'm fine, I think that's then where the problems can come." In this way, engagement could be seen as indicative of parents' commitment to good parenting. Also referring to parental engagement a team manager (LA 14) stated: "I would say, with young mums, [at] some point during the pregnancy where they've just realised that actually they can't do this, and you can see that, that sort of shutdown, where they stop engaging with services and they start re-engaging with really harmful risky behaviours."

A senior practitioner (LA 8) stated that she was often "brutally honest" and advised parents in and leaving care to "play the game, jump through the hoops, do whatever is asked of you by the social worker, you know, be honest with them, tell them if you've got any anxieties or fears, do all that". Reflecting on a positive example of such engagement, the team manager in LA 12 stated that the mother had responded to professional concerns with: "sheer determination, like 'You're not having this baby off me, he is mine and I'm going to have it and I'm going to love it and you tell me what to do, I'll do it and I will prove you all wrong.'" Similarly, the team manager in LA 4 stated:

> 'She was a very stubborn young person and I think she just thought, do you know what, I am going to prove myself to you, and she absolutely did, she engaged with everything in terms of health services, she went to college, she maintained all of her appointments, she went to parenting classes, she did absolutely everything ... and in the end even like the police were saying there's literally no more we can ask this girl to do.'

The comments quoted in this section emphasise that, despite adversity and disadvantage, parenting is possible for young people in and leaving care. Individual factors are viewed as highly influential in determining outcomes and trajectories; namely young people's willingness to engage with professionals, take on board advice and "do whatever is asked". The extent to which such expectations apply only to care-experienced parents is unclear. For example, willingness to engage with professionals and commitment to positive parenting and lifestyles would likely be important for any parent subject to safeguarding concerns. However, it is also possible that parents in and leaving care face additional expectations, influenced by stigmatised and discriminatory practices (see Chapter 4). In this way, advice to "play the game" and "jump through the hoops" may be reflective of a subtle but important practice shift whereby parents are expected to proactively prove parenting ability, rather than experiencing social work involvement when there is evidence of abuse or neglect. In addition, the propensity to frame outcomes and trajectories as within individuals' choice and control, downplays the responsibilities of the state as parent and the potential for multiple and multifaceted support needs. As detailed in Chapter 5, parents in and leaving care can be highly motivated to be better and do better as parents; however, the extent to which this is possible and realistic needs to be considered in the context of their circumstances and resources. As argued by Dominelli et al (2005: 1133) 'Failing to connect personal capacities to structural inequalities and leaving mothers and children unsupported and without adequate resources ... make[s] failure the most likely outcome regardless of personal aspirations.'

Informal support: having someone by your side

In addition to personal determination and willingness to engage with professionals, a young person's support network was seen as a key factor influencing parenting outcomes. As noted in the previous section, professionals repeatedly recognised the demands and challenges of parenting and, as such, believed that the availability of reliable, consistent, nurturing support was a key factor in determining outcomes. For example, the senior practitioner from LA 9 stated: "it's having that person isn't it, that is literally by your side because [being a new parent] is the hardest thing you'll ever know isn't it?" Potential sources of support included partners, partner's families, former foster carers as well as birth families:

> 'If they're actually in a relationship, not on their own, if they've got somebody that's there to support them that's massive.' (Senior practitioner LA 2)

> 'If they've got some trusting adults in their life who are there to call on, perhaps on a Saturday afternoon if something has gone wrong or they're struggling, that makes things much more successful ... whether it's some distant aunty who is nice and caring and stuff, that can make a massive difference. ... [Q]uite often, if we get a looked after young person who is in a relationship with a dad who is from a

lovely family environment, the mum can see all that and if they take her under their wing, which I have noticed has happened before, and they sort of mother her as well and then they've played the grandparent role but quite a heightened grandparent role, that can work very successfully for the youngster.' (Team manager LA 5)

'Sometimes those are cases where the young person has had a, been in a long-term foster placement, they've got someone they can rely on. I know of cases where the young person had continued to live with the foster carer, you know, thinks of that foster parent as a, you know, very much as a biological attachment I suppose, and has had a child there and been supported, those have worked out. There have been others where, you know, the young woman has met somebody who is quite stable and/or has a stable family that can support them and help them and I think those cases can work. … And I can think of cases where actually, even if the young person, the young woman isn't, you know, back living with the original birth parents, they're still, kind of things have moved on and they're able to assist now.' (Team manager LA 19)

These accounts suggest that informal support may be available to young people from a range of sources, including partners and their families, former carers as well as birth family members. Early research from Quinton and Rutter (1984) lends some support to practitioners' reflections, as they found that women who grew up in care and had a supportive partner were no more likely than those who were not care-experienced to demonstrate poor parenting. In this study, practitioners did not portray a preference as to who provided support for young people, but simply that the availability of support could influence experiences and outcomes for parents in and leaving care. A team manager's (LA 5) reference to a heightened grandparent role is noteworthy, whereby nurturing support is available to the parent as well as the child. The importance of "mother[ing] the mother" has previously been argued by Rothenberg (2005: 24).

Interviews with parents revealed that support was sometimes available through the means suggested by professionals. For example, in the case of Zoe, relationships with her birth family had improved after she had her baby and she discussed having multiple people available for support. Talking about the location of her new property she stated:

'[I]t is like [the] ideal location. My mum is right by there, my mum is like three streets down. Then my boyfriend's mother is just down the road. I'm friends with the next door neighbour. It's because I grew up around here. My foster carer is literally like at the bottom of this road, she's like further down you know it's brilliant. It is like the ideal location for me, I love it yeah.' (Zoe)

For Zoe, there was no shortage of people to turn to for advice and support. Zoe felt multiple trusted individuals were close by to help her if and when needed. Yet in other examples, parents had few, if any, individuals they could rely on, and support from key individuals had the potential to be temporary, unreliable or unsuitable. For example, while valuable support could be provided from partners and their families, this was sometimes only available for the duration of the relationship. In Zoe's follow-up interview, her relationship with her partner had ended and she reflected that his mother "doesn't really speak to me now. If I see her out she will ask how [child's name] is but she doesn't see her." Similarly, during her first interview Rebecca stated she could go to her partner's mother "for anything. She's been more of a mother to me than my own." However, at the point of her second interview, her relationship with her partner had ended, and the relationship with his mother had deteriorated to hostile rather than supportive. While Zoe had other supportive figures to rely on, this was not the case for Rebecca. For example, in contrast to Zoe describing her former foster carer as being at the end of the road, Rebecca stated: "I have a good relationship with one of my carers but I haven't talked to her in months now because we got our own things going on." While Rebecca spoke very highly of her former foster carer, crediting her with "saving her life", their relationship following her transition to independent living was described in more distant terms, rather than offering regular or consistent support.

Support from birth families was also described as problematic. For example, Tara stated that her mother had repeatedly promised to visit her when she had her baby, but never had and added: "My sister was meant to have [child's name] every other weekend just to give me a break. But she didn't stick to that." In other instances, historical or ongoing concerns about birth family members prevented support being accessed. When asked if she had anyone available for support, Charlotte responded: "No because my mum is an alcoholic, my stepfather is disabled and so no, there's no one on my side of the family I can turn to."

While Charlotte had restricted access between her mother and child, in some instances parents had been directed by Children's Services to prohibit contact. For example, James stated: "They [social services] said, no matter what happens, your parents aren't going to be able to go anywhere near [child's name]. And I felt that quite unfair to be honest because my mum wasn't a problem, it was my father that was the problem, and my mum's ex-partner."

In a similar example, Emma discussed her frustration that her father was not allowed contact with her child even though he was not considered a risk to other children within the family. For James and Emma, the imposed conditions were regarded as unnecessary and unhelpful; further constraining their limited supportive options. While the rationale for such decisions is unknown, it is important to note the potential of the state to encourage as well as curtail informal support opportunities for parents in and leaving care.

These accounts demonstrate the potential for parents in and leaving care to have access to a range of people offering informal support, which they can rely on in times of need. It is possible that young people's relationships with birth family members will have resumed or improved, connections with carers will have been maintained, and new bonds forged with partners and their families. Yet, while such relationships may be both possible and desirable, the comments also demonstrate that such support is not the experience of all parents. For some, challenges with family relationships remain, relationships with carers diminish and support availability from partners and their families is unstable. In such cases, parents in and leaving care may be more heavily reliant on support from the state as parent. Similarly, as noted by Biehal and Wade (1996) insufficient informal support increases reliance on formal support. The following section will explore the possibilities available for parents wholly or partially reliant on the state for support.

Formal support: availability, acceptability and adequacy

In accordance with the potential for multiple and multifaceted needs, a range of formal supports and interventions were discussed by professionals, with service provision encompassing interventions spanning the continuum and four-tier model of services (Social Care Institute of Excellence 2012; Welsh Government 2017). These included references to universal services such as midwife and health visitor support, as well as mother and baby groups available within the local community. In addition, some participants discussed area-based provision targeted at families living in disadvantaged areas, and in some areas, projects specifically targeted at young parents were available, offering a range of individual and group support. Dependent on need, support provisions could also be accessed via Children's Services referrals. They included a number of interventions, varying in length, mode of delivery and focus, delivered by both the statutory and the third sector. In some instances, statutory process had been instigated, including child protection procedures and care proceedings.

Support provisions were typically available to a wide range of parents and were not specifically designed for or targeted at those in and leaving care. While these types of provisions constituted the bulk of provision discussed by professionals, there was widespread agreement that additional support was sometimes needed which took account of or was responsive to young people's care experience. Primarily, such support was available through leaving-care professionals; however, over the course of the study a variety of initiatives were discussed including:

- specialist advocacy support;
- therapeutic support offered during pregnancy;
- enhanced midwife and health visitor support for pregnant and new parents in and leaving care;
- parent and child placements (including parent and child foster placements, as well as supported living facilities, available within and outside of the local authority area);
- 'live-in' parenting support (this involved support workers providing up to 24-hour support to parents in their own tenancies, with support being reduced in accordance with individual needs);
- parenting courses, supper clubs and mother and baby groups facilitated by the leaving-care service;
- linking parents with foster carers, peer mentors or volunteers to provide flexible, tailored support.

While seemingly offering a range of options, the availability or use of such initiatives was highly variable across local authorities. For example, only in two interviews did professionals discuss routinely encouraging pregnant and parenting young people to consider independent advocacy support. Similarly, enhanced midwife support was available in some authorities, although only one was specifically targeted at care-experienced young people. At the time of data collection, one local authority was trialling a project whereby care-experienced young people were offered therapeutic support during pregnancy, with the aim of helping to address issues with the past and support their transition to parenthood. Initiatives such as peer and volunteer support schemes were on occasion described as 'in development', while parenting courses and mother and baby groups, delivered by the leaving-care team, were available in a small number of areas on an 'ad hoc' basis, or had been delivered previously as a 'one off'.

At the time of data collection, the National Youth Advocacy Service was piloting Project Unity – a holistic, wrap-around support service for care-experienced young mothers. Since the conclusion of the research, the pilot has received funding to deliver the service across Wales (National Youth Advocacy Service 2019). Although yet to be evaluated, it is hoped that the nationally available provision will ensure greater consistency in support for parents in and leaving care in Wales.

In addition to inconsistencies and uncertainties in targeted support availability, multiple challenges and barriers were identified by professionals with respect to ensuring adequate support for parents in and leaving care. The availability of appropriate housing was described as particularly problematic; simultaneously depicted as a fundamental need but also a scarcely available resource:

> 'Accommodation is a big issue. I think, you know, getting somebody into safe and secure permanent accommodation is huge, that provides the stability. … Like having a pushchair and then living in a house that's got about a hundred steps up the front of it, you know, it's difficult isn't it? And that's when things start to go wrong and so it's making sure that they've not only got accommodation but it's accommodation that suits them and enables them.' (Team manager LA 16)

> 'You know it's out of a young person's control, basically, the accommodation they're provided with, yeah. Yeah some of the places are pretty grim.' (Team manager LA 6)

As noted by the team manager in LA 16, the accommodation provided to young people has the potential to support parenting and provide a valuable foundation for 'success'. However, as highlighted in the example of Nic earlier in this chapter, inadequate and inappropriate accommodation also has the potential to amplify struggles and add to difficulties. Tasha similarly discussed her experience of being placed in hostels and trying to create a home for her daughter within an environment that included violence, criminal behaviour and drug use. While Tasha had been supported into more permanent accommodation, she stated that her current property was 'not a nice place' and was in poor condition.

For parents needing supported rather than independent accommodation, there were challenges with regard to availability as well as affordability. While some areas had some 'in-house' parent and child placements available with local authority carers, in other examples, young people were required to move considerable distances away and placements incurred considerable expense:

> 'We have got mother and baby provision but it's less available. I think it's, it's more available if we're into serious concerns about the child [rather than] to just give that additional bit of support.' (Team manager LA 5)

> 'The difficulty with [parent and child placements] is that they're so far away and so you're taking young people out of everything they know.' (Team manager LA 10)

In addition to uncertain availability, tensions were also apparent with regard to the support that was possible to provide, with multiple challenges acknowledged in efforts to develop services and ensure appropriate support for parents in and leaving care. For example, in addition to concerns about dual responsibilities and divided loyalties (discussed in Chapter 4), leaving-care professionals were also considered well placed to support parents; but their ability to provide additional help or respond to increased needs was problematic due to limited professional capacity:

> 'I feel that our kids need a lot of support and we don't have enough time. [Referring to one father she was supporting] … I've seen him three times this week, you know, and he phones me up about everything … but, you know, I've got like 20 other kids, do you know what I mean?' (Senior practitioner LA 4)

Further practical difficulties were discussed with regard to facilitating group sessions. This was particularly difficult for parents living outside of major towns and cities: "The geography of the county doesn't help with doing group work, it takes you all your time to get young people into one place" (Senior practitioner LA 7). While this senior practitioner was discussing the challenges of coordinating group sessions across a largely rural area, these options were also difficult to access for young people who, for whatever reason, were living in a different local authority area to their respective leaving-care team. Rather than young people being transferred to the local authority in which they were resident, their original local authority continued to oversee their leaving-care provision. For some young people, this curtails the support that is available and can create additional barriers in navigating available provision.

The sustainability of support initiatives was also considered potentially problematic due to changeable numbers of pregnant and parenting young people. As noted by one senior practitioner (LA 17):

> 'We go through little cohorts ... so at some point we'll have, you know, maybe x number of parents going on at the same time and then at other times we might have, you know, a couple of pregnancies. ... [I]t's not like you have such significant numbers that you can systematically think this is a service that we're going to need to provide now. And I think that's probably one of the stumbling blocks.'

The comments from the senior practitioner highlight similar challenges to those noted in Chapter 2; ever scarce financial resources require difficult decisions to be made with respect to support availability. In this example, committing funding to an issue of fluctuating demand was difficult to prioritise.

These reflections highlight multiple and multifaceted barriers inhibiting the development and delivery of support for parents in and leaving care. Adding to the complexity, concerns were also expressed with regard to the support that should be offered, for how long and for what purpose. For example, facilitating groups specifically for care-experienced parents was a contentious issue; with some professionals believing the development of such groups to be stigmatising, compounding notions that parents in and leaving care were likely to be struggling as parents. However, in other interviews, opportunities for parents to meet others with shared understanding of the care system were viewed as providing valuable opportunities for peer support while minimising anxieties and feelings of difference:

> '[Young parents in and leaving care] feel a bit conscious about attending some of those [universal services] because they are generally older parents who have got a good social network and they feel as though everyone is looking at them

if they turn up, and feel as though they're being judged and watched.' (Social worker LA 18)

Related to this, concerns were expressed as to the nature of support and whether it was primarily designed to provide meaningful help or to monitor/assess parents: "Young parents coming through the system – it doesn't feel like support, it sounds awful, yeah, it does feel almost like policing, [they are] being watched and it's token positive: 'Oh she is engaging well with social services BUT …'" (Personal adviser LA 22). Likewise, the expectation for support provision to be temporary and to address needs in the short term was also subject to criticism:

> 'There seems to be a reluctance to accept that some parents, including those with challenging childhood experiences, learning disabilities, etc., will need long-term support. For some this will mean long-term 24-hour support. As a society there seems to be a reluctance to accept this type of dependency or need.' (Senior manager LA 6)

Such comments echo previous criticisms by Featherstone et al (2014: 137), who note the 'absence of relationship building with families, with repeated short-term interventions'.

Overall, professionals were largely critical of the support available to parents in and leaving care, and the ability of the state as parent to replicate the type of support typically expected of grandparents:

> 'I think we'd have to look at the sorts of services that normal everyday grandparents provide, general support, kind of babysitting, helping out financially now and again, just the sort of stuff that we, as a council, don't do.' (Team manager LA 10)

> 'Yeah, I think [corporate parents] need to have a better understanding and recognition in terms of what they would do for their own children when they're a parent, the support that they would provide. … I guess it's those little things that a lot people take for granted that care leavers don't have the opportunity to have really, which makes it twice as hard for them.' (Senior practitioner LA 20)

In summary, for parents reliant on formal support provision, there is variability in the support that is available and substantial barriers to developing responses that meet the range of practical, emotional and financial needs identified. While positive progress has recently been observed in Wales (National Youth Advocacy Service 2019) with respect to ensuring greater consistency of support for parents in and leaving care, it is nevertheless important to highlight the mismatch between the range of potential needs identified for care-experienced parents with the uncertain support options and their perceived inadequacy. Similarly, the data suggests that responding to the spectrum of potential needs identified in this section extend far beyond the remit of one agency and necessitate commitment and cooperation from all corporate parenting agencies.

As a starting point for developing support responses, the following section explores parents' experiences of support and intervention.

Experiences of support: personalised options, 'voluntary' engagement and perceived benefit

For parents who had experiences of formal support, there was a mixture of opinions as to its adequacy and influence. For example, Amy was referred to a parenting course and reflected positively on its impact:

> 'It gave me a sense of routine, it gave me a sense of empathy towards your own child. … I didn't have the emotional support to become a mum at that time and I think that having the parenting course gave me that, it gave me the emotional support, and confidence as well to put everything into that routine.'

Zoe similarly spoke warmly about her experiences of a young parents group, valuing the informal opportunity to create and maintain friendships:

> 'Yeah it's like, it's kind of like, it's a mother and baby group, they have like a massive play mat thing in the middle, they do like cups of tea, squash and like biscuits and stuff. And all the babies just like play together with the toys and like most of the mothers we just have a chat really, just a catch-up and see how things are going.'

Other parents also reflected positively on services for young parents, commenting both on the range of support available, as well as the relationships with individual staff members. For example, Leah reflected on the opportunities she had had to learn about healthy relationships, engage with baby massage sessions, as well as attend parent and child groups. Positive comments were also made by Matt and Tina. As noted in Chapter 5, Matt and Tina had strained relationships with social workers and carers and believed that professionals wanted them to fail. In contrast, the couple had forged more trusting relationships with staff at the service, believing they were "different" and felt that they could talk through issues with certain staff members.

Several participants reflected positively on the Unity project (National Youth Advocacy Service 2019), valuing the mix of practical and emotional support, the flexible nature of the service and the development of a trusting relationship with the keyworker. Consistent with the range of needs identified earlier in this chapter, support encompassed help with finances, housing, health, as well as engaging with social workers and other professionals. Reflecting on her relationship with her keyworker, Kim stated: "I think everyone should have a [keyworker's name]. She been there for me when I've needed her. She believed in me and I felt like she was on my side." Sophie similarly referred to feeling the Unity worker was "on her side" and stated she considered their relationship more akin to a friendship than a professional one. In another example, Molly was positive about the support available to her from Unity, as well as the comprehensive package of support that had been offered to her by Children's Services. This included an array of services designed to address mental health needs, to develop parenting skills and ward against unhealthy relationships. "They [Children's Services] had everything in place and said it was my choice. … [T]hey were there when I needed them, they've been brilliant. … I find that they've been very supportive and helpful."

These findings incorporate support from the statutory and voluntary sector, and include universal, targeted and more intensive interventions. Key to the positive reflections by parents appeared to be the approach and relationships with key professionals, the level of choice and control afforded to them in terms of accessing support, as well as the perceived benefits of engagement.

In contrast to the positive reflections quoted so far in this section, other parents were more critical of the support that had been offered to them. This included accusations of inadequate, unhelpful and overly harsh interventions. Some reflected that little support was available from social workers and connected professionals. For example, Aaron became a father at 17 and reflected that he felt ill-prepared for what was to come:

> 'I don't know, like, being a, like being a child in care, I think I should have got a lot more support from the local authority but I haven't. … I've had like five different social workers [in the last year] and, like, not one of them has, like, tried to sit me down and speak to me about what being a parent was going to be like, because I didn't really know what it was going to be like, like it didn't really seem real to me.'

While Aaron felt that more preparatory support should have been available prior to his child's birth, Sarah stated she had been struggling to manage as a single mother but did not receive support when she asked social workers for help: "I phoned social services, I was crying, I said 'I need help, I need some support, I just feel like killing myself.' That was it, they came out, they said you're incapable this that and the other and they took her and off they went."

Related to this, Tasha stated she frequently felt penalised rather than supported by professionals. Tasha stated that she confided in professionals that she felt low due to the demands of caring for a baby. She stated that this information was later referred to in care proceedings to imply that her mental health posed a potential risk to her daughter. In another example, she stated that she was forced to end her relationship after disclosing her partner had experienced a lapse in drug use. The subsequent restrictions on contact between her daughter and her partner meant she had even fewer opportunities to access help with caring, circumstances that she felt were likely to exacerbate mental health difficulties:

> 'I won't ask them for nothing. Every time my life is going good and things are ok they will come and fuck it up. … I've jumped through every hoop, done everything they wanted and still they won't leave me alone. They fucked up my childhood, I don't want them anywhere near my daughter. They lie, don't do what they say they'll do, or do what they say they won't do, mess people's lives up, nothing ever gets done about it.'

The examples given are indicative of the diversity in young people's needs and experiences. Some young people felt supported and were positive about professional involvement, while others harboured strong feelings of anger and resentment. As noted in previous chapters, it is not the intention of this book to provide analysis of individual situations and trajectories. It is recognised that the reflections of individuals offer valuable but nonetheless partial insights, and the perspectives of connected parties may differ from those presented here. Nevertheless, the reflections of parents are consistent with previous comments emphasising the importance of positive professional relationships as well as concerns about stigma, discrimination and disadvantage (Chapters 4 and 5). Similarly, the reflections help illuminate the challenges noted by professionals quoted earlier, who respond to diverse needs as well as manage risk, and ensure supportive responses that are both wanted and available.

Consistent with this, concerns were evident in the extent to which support was voluntary or compulsory, and whether it was designed primarily to monitor and assess, or provide support. For example, in contrast to Zoe's positive experience of a young parents group, Sophie felt compelled to attend a similar group, with her attendance monitored and reported back to the social worker:

> 'Yeah [if I didn't go] it would get reported back to like [social worker] that I didn't go. ... It's good in a way because it gets me out of the house and it is good for X and it's good for me to get out. But sometimes I feel like I like to stay in and chill and do all the housework and stuff. ... It's just like, it's, I'm so busy and like always tired because I'm so busy.'

While Sophie recognised positive benefits of attending the group, feeling pressured to attend also had the potential to increase stress and resentment. In a similar example Kim stated: "I find it can be too much sometimes, I am bombarded with like support and you can do this, you can do that, you can do. ... I don't want to do it. It is too much so, yeah, I find I'm too bombarded with too much sometimes."

During her interview Kim complained that she had multiple people visiting the house and was also encouraged to attend a variety of group sessions. In addition to feeling pressured to accept the support offered and fearful of the consequences of refusing, the support available did not correspond with what she felt was needed. Kim had no family to turn to and had sometimes struggled without a break. Ironically, the frequency of appointments and visits had exacerbated these difficulties: "They say 'sleep when the baby sleeps', well that's not possible when there's people always coming." Yet despite feeling 'support' was overwhelming and unhelpful, some parents feared the consequences of refusing the help available:

> 'I've had parenting classes, baby massage, breast feeding support, mother and baby groups, healthy eating and cooking. Some of it was ok, but some I really didn't need. It adds extra stress but you have to do what they say or they'll take the baby. That's how it feels and that's how it is. The minute you say no they say "We'll look at child protection again."' (Anna)

These accounts suggest that parents were sometimes pressured to engage in support, and this was at odds with what parents wanted and believed helpful. Related to this, concerns about the purpose of support were apparent. The following parents spent time in mother and baby units and felt the emphasis was on monitoring and assessment as opposed to encouragement and support:

> 'I went into a mother and baby placement. I didn't like it, it was like living in the Big Brother house … they were over you 24/7. If I went anywhere in the house with the baby I had to take the baby monitor with me. The foster carer had to have the other one.' (Leanne)

> 'If you wanted to take your child upstairs, if you wanted to bath your child, you had to be watched … like you are some sort of paedophile. Am I a criminal now that I've had a baby?' (Emma)

> 'I have spent longer than anyone in mother and baby [units]. I was in one first, passed that all good, perfect report. Then they said the staff had gotten too close to us and weren't independent. Then I had to go to another one. At that one the cameras were on all the time, they watched everything. They even wanted to watch me breastfeeding. I had to fight and get my advocate to say "You are not watching me while I'm undressed!"' (Tasha)

In contrast to mother and baby placements providing opportunities for comprehensive advice and support, the comments of Leanne, Emma and Tasha suggest they were treated with suspicion, with mechanisms designed to monitor and manage risk. Such comments resonate with those in the previous chapter, where parents felt stigmatised and negatively judged by professionals. The comments can also be related to Luke and Sebba's (2014) review of the evidence with respect to parent and child foster placements, which highlighted the importance of clearly defined roles, positive relationships with carers and young people feeling emotionally and practically supported.

Overall, these comments highlight the potential for support to be perceived as enforced, overbearing and unhelpful. In seeking to understand parents' negative experiences, the comments may be reflective of inaccurate understandings of needs, concerns to manage risk as well as respond to needs, and/or a mismatch between the support needs identified and the support services available. It is also important to note that, despite the acknowledged importance of having a break from parenting, the services described did not encompass such provision. Related to this, the comments may be indicative of the disparity in responses and expectations for care-experienced parents. Professional emphasis on the importance of engaging with professionals, notions of "doing whatever is necessary" and "playing the game", may be reflective of expectations to prove parenting capacity (see Chapter 4). Likewise, support options offered to young people may be shaped by priorities and motives which may or may not be known to young people. For example, engagement with an array of available support may help ease safeguarding concerns and ensure that children are regularly monitored. While acknowledging such possibilities and complexity, it is also important to consider the impact and experience of such approaches, including the extent to which responses are fair and consistent with needs, are reflective of expectations and support availability for other parents, and whether they encourage parenting 'success'.

Discussion: diverse needs, passive corporate parents and absent corporate grandparents

The in-depth consideration of support in this chapter, provides valuable context for understanding parenting outcomes and provides a necessary foundation from which to consider further development. First, the findings highlight the potential for multiple and multifaceted needs; needs which reflect the challenging and demanding nature of parenting, as well as those connected to experiences before, during or while leaving care. While there is no suggestion that all parents in and leaving care will have intensive or long-term difficulties, professionals and parents in this study identified a range of potential support considerations.

Despite the range of practical, emotional and financial support needs acknowledged, professionals believed that parenthood was possible if parents were prepared to do "whatever is required". Typically, this meant engaging with professionals, evidencing personal responsibility and demonstrating a commitment to positive parenting. Repeated references were made to resilience and determination, and examples of young people who had proved themselves as parents, in spite of significant adversity. While the achievements of young people are rightly applauded, the emphasis on individual attitude and behaviour considerably downplays the extent to which the needs highlighted for parents might be considered part of the responsibilities of the state as parent.

In addition to individual factors, professionals also made repeated references to young people's resources and the availability of support. Informal support resources were viewed as highly influential over the experiences and trajectories of parents. While some parents enjoyed the support of partners, family members and carers, for others, having 'someone by your side' and the availability of practical, emotional or financial help was not possible or reliable from connected figures. Biehal and Wade (1996) previously found little evidence of efforts to boost or facilitate informal supports. While Aparicio et al (2015: 53) advocated 'seizing the opportunity for strengthening support and rebuilding family connections', the findings of this study continue to suggest a passive corporate parent approach, whereby the support of partners, family members, carers and friends, is hoped for and preferable, but not routinely or actively sought.

Compounding the potential for disadvantage, the findings suggested that access to and experiences of formal support was variable. Approaches remain underdeveloped due to challenges with respect to acceptability, feasibility and sustainability; factors which further perpetuate difficulties associated with generating evidence of impact and good practice models of support (Finnigan-Carr et al 2015). While acknowledging examples of initiatives which seek to forge positive relationships with parents, develop skills and respond to diverse needs, the availability of supportive approaches was inconsistent. Moreover, professional and parent perspectives typically suggested support responses to be insufficient, with the support available from the state as parent considered a poor substitute compared to that typically expected from grandparents. Tensions are evident in the extent to which support corresponds to parents' needs and preferences, is perceived as compulsory or voluntary, and whether it is designed primarily to monitor and assess or to provide meaningful help. The findings chime with Featherstone et al's (2018) depiction of 'high challenge/low support approaches' and suggest little progress has been made, despite the wider literature consistently noting the need for broad support responses encompassing housing, finances, mental and physical health, and social support (Mendes 2009; Connolly et al 2012; Svoboda et al 2012).

Conclusion

In conclusion, the Voices study has highlighted a mismatch between support needs and availability for parents in and leaving care. The findings presented suggest a disproportionate emphasis on individual factors and overly optimistic reliance on the availability of informal support, combined with underdeveloped responses from the state as parent. The extent to which the responsibilities of the state as parent can and should extend to those of grandparent has received insufficient consideration and there is a lack of consensus as to what support should be available, for how long and for what purpose. Despite some promising service developments (National Youth Advocacy Service 2019), practice experience of fluctuating demand and variable needs and preferences, combined with ever pressured resources and funds, has largely hindered progress and impeded the development of corporate parenting responses. As such, challenges with respect to generating evidence of effectiveness and models of good practice remain (Mullins et al 2014; Fallon and Broadhurst 2015; Finnigan-Carr et al 2015). The findings confirm the urgent need for policy and practice attention at the national, local and personal levels (Bullock et al 2006). Considerations of what such attention could and should entail will be considered in the following and final chapter.

Acknowledgements

Table 6.1 was originally published in Roberts, L., Maxwell, N. and Elliott, M. (2019) 'When young people in and leaving state care become parents: What happens and why?', *Children and Youth Services Review*, 104: 104387.

7

Conclusion: if this were my child

This book was intended to provide a holistic consideration of pregnancy and parenthood for young people in and leaving care. The preceding chapters have provided evidence of outcomes, considered available support and offered insight into the perspectives of parents and professionals. In accordance with the initial aims, the book has shone a light on this important but neglected area of practice, provided a platform for parents' views and perspectives, and considered how their experiences are both shaped and influenced by their care status. This final chapter draws together key findings from the Voices research and revisits recurring questions and concerns discussed at the outset. In seeking to fulfil the final aim of the book to be a resource for policy and practice professionals, the chapter offers a series of recommendations, co-produced with young people, parents and professionals. The chapter concludes with a section written by a member of the parents' advisory group, who offers a final plea for meaningful policy and practice change.

Summary points

This section is intended to provide a condensed overview of the stand-out findings from the preceding chapters and revisits salient points from each of the three thematic sections: outcomes (Chapters 2 and 3), experiences (Chapters 4 and 5) and support (Chapter 6).

Outcomes: care-experienced young people face increased likelihood of early pregnancy and parenthood

- International evidence has long suggested young people in and leaving care are at risk of early pregnancy.
- Secondary analysis of the School Health Research Network surveys (2015, 2017) showed disparities in sexual health outcomes for care-experienced young people.
- Professionals acknowledged a heightened risk of early pregnancy. Despite expressing some confidence in the care system to meet young

people's sexual health and development needs, barriers to effective practice included cuts to funding and services, an absence of official guidance and a belief that, for some young people, early pregnancy and parenthood was an unfortunate but inevitable trajectory.

Experiences: parents in and leaving care are vulnerable to considerable disadvantage and adversity

- There is potential for parents in and leaving care to experience multiple and multifaceted needs. These included needs connected to parenting, as well as challenges with respect to housing, health, finances, relationships and independent living skills.
- Despite wanting to be better and do better for their children, almost all parents were worried about social workers. Rather than seeing professionals as having corporate parenting responsibilities towards them, as individuals who could help, social workers were often talked about as adding to problems or making difficulties worse. Many thought social workers judged them because of the past and thought they were going to be like their parents.
- Consistent with this, professionals acknowledged being concerned about the impact of young people's experiences on their ability to be 'good' parents.
- Practices such as routine referral of parents for Children's Services assessment as well unfettered access to historical records mean that parents are treated differently because of their care status.

Support: support for parents in and leaving care is variable and underdeveloped

- Despite leaving-care professionals wanting and trying to support parents, relationships with young people were sometimes hindered by high workloads, as well as competing obligations to share information with other social workers and follow child protection procedures.
- Support from corporate parents was variable across areas and didn't always correspond to what parents needed or wanted. Overall, the support available did not reflect the type of help that would ordinarily be expected from grandparents.
- There are barriers to developing and improving support availability because:
  - little evidence exists with respect to what support is wanted or effective;

- support needs for parents and children are both variable and changeable;
- service demand is changeable and commitment of ever scarce resources is difficult to justify;
- there is disagreement over the extent to which targeted support is seen as helpful or stigmatising.

Outcomes: parents in and leaving care face increased risk of Children's Services intervention and separation from children

- High rates of intervention and separation were found in the Voices study, with one in four children (26 per cent) captured in the survey separated from both birth parents.
- Secondary analysis of the Wales Adoption Study similarly showed that care-experienced parents were over-represented among birth parents whose children were being placed for adoption.
- The findings are consistent with international evidence and add to the developing evidence with respect to increased risk of poor outcomes for parents in and leaving care.

Recurring themes and questions revisited

'Success' for parents in and leaving care

Over the course of the book, notions of success have been explored from a variety of perspectives; thought of in terms of outcomes, as well as experience, and considered from the position of the individual, as well as from the perspective of the state as parent.

First, it is important to recognise the 'success' of individual young people who retain care for their children, often in spite of significant adversity. While some of the parents featured in the Voices research were fortunate to have access to formal and informal resources, others faced perpetual struggle, experienced multiple and multifaceted needs, intensified by minimal, temporary or unstable opportunities for support. Parents' resilience and ability to withstand intense scrutiny and uncertainty is inspiring and should be applauded.

Despite this, conceiving of success as reflective of individual choices and personal responsibility insufficiently recognises the extent to which 'success' for parents in and leaving care is inextricably connected to and reflective of, the actions of the state as parent. In terms of planning for parenthood, evidence has long indicated the increased risk of early pregnancy for young people who are 'looked after'. Yet policy and practice guidance is underdeveloped and relentless financial pressures have impeded service delivery. Moreover, evidence suggesting that young people can be left languishing in poverty, in uncertain and/or unsuitable accommodation, combined with professional support that is paralysed by limited capacity, scarce resources and tensions of dual roles and competing responsibilities, suggests an endemic failure to provide the foundations for parenting 'success'. Disproportionate rates of intervention and separation, underdeveloped and/or discriminatory state responses, as well as broad acknowledgement that support from corporate parents is a poor substitute for support typically expected from grandparents, cannot and should not be explained away as individuals not 'wanting it enough' or being insufficiently determined, unwilling to engage or unable to put the needs of the child before their own. Rather, notions of 'success' for parents in and leaving care should be considered indicative, at least in part, of the actions and care of the state as parent. As argued by Mendes et al (2014), if authoritative state intervention into family life is to be justified, there is a moral obligation to ensure that children's and young people's outcomes are better as a result. Prioritising 'success' in future family life, when this was not possible in childhood, arguably provides an important benchmark for reflection and evaluation of state intervention.

The relationship between the state as parent, and parents in and leaving care

Relationships between parents and professionals, in particular regarding expectations and understandings of roles, responsibilities and motives, have been recurrent themes over the course of this book. How professionals perceived and engaged with parents in and leaving care, how parents perceived and responded to professionals and the ways in which relationships are forged and navigated within the confines of statutory roles and processes, were repeatedly discernible within individual reflections. Leaving-care professionals were often cognisant of their corporate parenting role, yet their perspectives did not suggest shared understanding and commitment among wider professionals. Likewise, while recognising their parenting responsibilities, leaving-care professionals were conscious of the limitations and deficits of the system in responding to the needs of young people as parents. For parents, notions of statutory professionals as corporate parents were often not discernible. To varying degrees, in young people's interactions with the state, the state was understood as responsive, intrusive, neglectful and punitive.

The different conceptualisations of the relationship between parents in and leaving care and the state as parent map onto Fox Harding's (1997) classic value perspectives typology. Although Fox Harding was concerned more broadly with the relationship between the state and the family, her theory is nevertheless helpful in conceptualising the nature and purpose of state intervention and involvement with parents in and leaving care, with all four perspectives discernible over the course of the research. For example, the absence of policy and practice guidance suggest a laissez-faire approach, supported also by parent and professional reflections of underdeveloped and neglected opportunities for support. In addition, the role as the state to protect children is visible. Evidence of disproportionate rates of intervention and separation, combined with routine referral of parents for assessment and dual responsibilities to safeguard as well as support, suggest the state as parent primed and ready to adopt a protectionist stance. In their reflections, parents' reported feeling investigated and monitored, and perceived intervention as unhelpful and punitive, as opposed to supportive. Related to this, there can also be a tendency to conceive of the needs of the child as separate to, or in conflict with, those of the parent. For young people with additional needs and vulnerabilities, the needs of the child can supersede the needs of the parent and/or the needs of the parent can be reframed in terms of risk to the child. More positively, attempts to support parents were recognised in the array of generic family support initiatives and there have been attempts also to develop tailored supports which recognise and respond to individual care experience. Notwithstanding challenges associated with capacity, sustainability, acceptability and availability, there was some evidence of individual, local and organisational efforts to encourage parents and support families.

While Fox Harding's (1997) typology insufficiently captures the role of the state as parent, the model is helpful in reflecting on current policy and practice. While the role of the state to protect children from abuse and neglect is constant, the findings of this research suggest there is broad scope for strengthening support for parents, challenging stigma and discrimination, and making explicit responsibilities and expectations with respect to good practice.

The findings of this study and previous literature suggest that leaving-care professionals conceive of themselves as the closest embodiment of young people's corporate parents (Rutman et al 2002). Despite being keenly aware of their responsibilities, professionals were hindered in their ability to fully support young people: impeded by limited resources and support availability, high workloads and sometimes competing obligations with respect to child protection. In addition to these challenges faced by leaving-care professionals, the findings of the research did not suggest any wider network of individuals and agencies explicitly and actively fulfilling their corporate parenting responsibilities. With varying degrees of success, leaving-care professionals frequently portrayed themselves as advocating on behalf of young people, attempting to challenge stigma and discrimination and/or working to ensure young people's rights and entitlements were respected. If young people in and leaving care are to be given the best chance of 'success', in parenting or otherwise, there should be broad commitment to revise and renew corporate parenting obligations.

To consider this further, Bullock et al (2006) conceptualise corporate parenting as 'an impersonal entity', with tasks shared between individuals and agencies, and delivered at national, local and individual levels. The analogy is helpful in highlighting the myriad of professionals and agencies with corporate parenting responsibilities that could be drawn on to strengthen support for parents in and leaving care. The conceptualisation illuminates the array of resources and connections the state as parent has at its disposal: far more than almost any individual parent. If utilised effectively, they offer some optimism for future policy and practice development, and ensuring holistic and comprehensive consideration of needs.

As detailed in the recommendations (one of the subsequent sections in this chapter), opportunities to address the issue of pregnancy and parenting for young people in and leaving care are broad and extend beyond professionals in direct contact with young people. However, in contrast to Bullock et al's (2006) notion of an 'impersonal' parent, it is also important to remember that parenting is not impersonal. On the contrary, it is deeply personal, and the behaviours, experiences, accomplishments and adversities faced by our children induce the strongest of emotions. Viewed in this way, efforts to provide substitute care for young people should seek to replicate a sense of care and commitment ordinarily expected within birth families. Encouragingly, in reference to young people transitioning from state care, the *Social Services and Wellbeing (Wales) Act 2014 Code of Practice* (Welsh Government 2018c: 79) states that 'all elected members and officers of the local authority, as corporate parents' operate under the principle of 'is this good enough for my child?' Comparable directions are evident in other UK nations (Department for Health, Social Services and Public Safety 2012; the Scottish Government 2015; Department for Education 2018a). It is unlikely that inaction with respect to risky sexual behaviours and early pregnancy, as well as uncertainty and inadequacy with regard to basics such as where to live and who to rely on for support would constitute 'good enough' for the majority of parents. Perpetual experiences of stigma, discrimination and disadvantage would not remain unchallenged. Likewise, confining help to within office hours and the dual concern to monitor as well as support, would be neither the experience, nor considered acceptable within the vast majority of birth families. In this way, it is hoped that the findings of this research warrant an emotional, as opposed to an impersonal reaction. There were undoubtedly glimpses of such emotions from some of the professionals who participated in the interviews; however this was often accompanied by a sense of powerlessness and impotence in addressing injustice.

In his discussion of successive reforms of Children's Services in England, Forrester (2016: 11) argues that attention has focused predominantly on the 'what' and 'when' of practice, rather than the 'why' and 'how'. The 'why' and 'how', he suggests (2016: 11) 'requires a vision for what children's service should be striving to achieve. This needs to include the core values of the organisation, the ultimate aims we might strive for and how we should work with families and children to achieve such goals.' When responding to pregnancy and parenthood for young people in and leaving care, it is imperative that we consider the why and how of practice. This should be based on a commitment to supporting young people through this major life event, aiming to replicate the type of support ordinarily expected from grandparents and to prevent intergenerational cycles of family separation. Such aspirations necessitate cooperation and commitment from all individuals and agencies with corporate parenting responsibilities.

Research strengths and limitations

Before making recommendations for policy and practice, it is appropriate to recognise both the strengths and limitations of the research presented.

The study was specifically concerned with the Welsh context and each of the 22 local authorities in Wales participated in one or more phases. Wales is an interesting and important context for research of this nature, considering its relatively large care population (McGhee et al. 2017). While consultations and discussions with key stakeholders outside of Wales suggest much overlap in practice and experience, it is also important to point to the divergence in legislation and policy, and to acknowledge that further research is needed to corroborate the findings across the UK nations.

The Voices study incorporated primary data from every local authority in Wales. The perspectives of professionals enabled insight into practice efforts to support parents in and leaving care as well as the tensions, challenges and restrictions inherent within the care system. Likewise, the reflections of parents have brought to life the hopes, anxieties, challenges and rewards of parenting; capturing both diversity and commonality in their experience. However, it should be noted that there was much variety in professionals' roles and responsibilities, and the data generated cannot be assumed to be representative of perspectives within teams or authorities. Similarly, parent participants were largely recruited through the support of third parties and the potential for bias is acknowledged. In addition, participants were predominantly mothers and the findings may inadequately reflect the needs and experiences of fathers.

Twenty out of the 22 local authorities in Wales participated in a survey about the young people currently eligible for support as a young person in or leaving care. This information provided an unprecedented snapshot of current parents and their children. When designing the survey for local authorities, it was intended that data would be obtained with the help of local authority data management professionals. Unfortunately, the complexity of the local authority systems and the absence of routinely collected data with respect to pregnancy and parenting meant that it was not possible to quickly extract the necessary information. It became apparent that the most efficient way to access the data was via team managers or social workers who knew the circumstances and histories of the young people and could access/provide the required information. This required further (and sometimes significant) time commitment from the social work teams and impacted on both participation and the speed with which data could be collected. In addition, there was variation in how local authorities were prepared to provide the information. In some instances, the team manager was the lead contact and provided information on behalf of the department. In other instances, individual social workers and personal advisers provided details for the parents on their caseload. On some occasions, data was provided during face-to-face meetings, whereas others chose to provide the information remotely. The potential for inaccuracies and incomplete data is recognised and the lack of systematic data collection means it is possible that the data presented is an under-representation of the parent population.

The Voices research was further enhanced by secondary analysis of existing national data sets: the School Health Research Network survey (data sets from 2015 and 2017) and the Wales Adoption Study. These data sets, as well as information yielded from official social work records, enabled large-scale consideration of young people's responses. However, it is important to note that neither of these studies was initially designed to investigate issues related to pregnancy and parenthood for young people in and leaving care. While helpful, the data available offered only partial insights. With regard to the School Health Research Network survey, the cross-sectional design means that causal relationships cannot be established and it is unclear whether the behaviours and outcomes for young people in care were influenced by experiences prior to or during care. It is possible that aspects of the care system could be strengthened to support better outcomes for young people, but it is also possible that risks associated with early pregnancy have been mitigated, rather than exacerbated, by admission into care. In addition, social work records analysed as part of the Wales Adoption Study contained frequent instances of missing data and greater consistency in reporting birth parents' care histories and legal status would have strengthened the analysis. Adoption was also the outcome experienced by all children within the sample. As such, the analysis can only make a contribution to what is known about a particular sub-set of care leaver parents: parents whose child goes on to be adopted.

Despite the acknowledged limitations, it is hoped that the combination of national statistics, professional insights and parental reflections provides a comprehensive and robust basis from which to consider ongoing policy and practice development.

Recommendations: ongoing policy and practice development

Collectively, the findings presented in this book highlight the potential for parents in and leaving care to experience multiple disadvantage and discrimination. They provide evidence of poor outcomes and underdeveloped support responses. The findings of the study warrant urgent policy and practice attention, at national, local and individual levels. This section offers a number of recommendations which have emerged from a series of consultations held with a variety of key stakeholders; namely professionals, parents and young people.

Discussions with care-experienced parents have provided invaluable advice with respect to the conduct of the study and the considerations of key findings. Likewise, professional expertise afforded vital insights from both the statutory and third sectors. In the later stages of the study, consultations with non-care-experienced individuals were also conducted. This included discussions with parents with experience of Children's Services intervention. In addition, a consultation session was held with young people with little or no contact with social workers. This consultation enabled a fresh perspective, untainted by knowledge or experience of the system.

In accordance with the underdeveloped nature of policy and practice for parents in and leaving care, combined with the diversity in parents' needs and circumstances, the following recommendations should be considered a starting point for ongoing development. The recommendations have implications for policy and practice at individual, local and national levels. Collectively, they are intended to clarify responsibilities and strengthen responses to parents in and leaving care, to encourage best practice and parity of provision, and challenge disadvantage and injustice for parents. However, it is also important to note that while findings of poor outcomes, discrimination and disadvantage undoubtedly warrant policy and practice attention, there is a balance to be struck in advocating for increased consideration of support needs and improved support responses for young people in and leaving care, without unwittingly stigmatising and further contributing to the perception that all care-experienced parents will experience social work intervention and/or poor outcomes as parents. As argued by Mannay et al (2019), there is a tendency to conceive of care-experienced children and young people as a static homogeneous group. The same tendency is likely to apply to parents. While this book has repeatedly argued that insufficient attention has been paid to this area, it would also seek to avoid developments which unhelpfully envisage parents as one group and make generalised assumptions about experiences, needs and interventions. The participants of the Voices research were diverse in their experiences of care and parenting, with both varying needs and available supports. One of the key challenges to ongoing development is accommodating this diversity.

National and local monitoring

National and local monitoring of numbers and outcomes, for pregnant and parenting young people in and leaving care is needed. The absence of official reporting has effectively shielded pregnancy and parenting for young people in and leaving care from policy and practice attention. Sustained recording and analysis would make clear the extent of support demand, highlight variations between local authorities, and provide an indication of the 'success' of corporate parents in preventing early pregnancy and avoiding intergenerational care experience. As stated in consultations with parents with experience of Children's Services intervention, statistics proving disproportionate rates of early pregnancy, parenthood and parent/child separation reflect poorly on the state as parent and provide an important impetus for positive change. Such action would also support policy initiatives in England and Wales to reduce the numbers of children and young people entering the care system and improve outcomes for those in care across the UK nations (Department for Health, Social Services and Public Safety 2012; Scottish Government 2015; Department for Education 2018a; Welsh Government 2018c).

Despite these advantages, consultations raised concerns about reducing young people's experiences to a statistic and the potential of such data to contribute further to stigmatised perceptions of care-experienced young people. The potential for such data collection to be temporary and/or to be released only within national and local working groups may resist such unintended consequences.

Practice guidance to support young people's sexual health and development

Practice guidance is needed to support the provision of sexual health advice and support for young people in care. Despite notions of shared responsibility and repeated opportunities to consider young people's needs and development, more work is needed to ensure that young people in and leaving care have access to sexual health advice and support. Practice guidance is needed to support professionals in this role, including providing clarification with respect to support for young people under the age of 16. Professionals should not be left to struggle with dilemmas in practice or to find themselves in contentious positions trying to reconcile responding to young people's needs with adhering to agency expectations. Information about contraception should form part of a wider programme of advice regarding healthy relationships and discussions about future family planning (i.e. encouraging thought and discussion about what circumstances they would like to be in before having a baby). While improving access to appropriate advice and support is important, so too is the need to ensure a sensitive approach that is likely to be acceptable to individual young people. For some, the privacy and confidentiality afforded by health professionals will be appealing, while for others confiding in an adult with whom they have an established and trusting relationship will be key. This person will vary in accordance with individual circumstances and relationships. However, consultations with care-experienced young people proposed that the social worker should take responsibility for overseeing the identification of this person and ensuring the provision of support.

> 'In the same way that I will make sure these conversations happen with my child, the social worker should be identifying the best person to talk to the young person, and making sure it happens.' (Advisory group member)

For such efforts to have the best chance of success, such initiatives should be developed in partnership with young people. Adopting a 'with young people' rather than 'for young people' approach will enable the most comprehensive consideration of ways to respond to known risks in relation to sexual health and early pregnancy but which avoid unwittingly stigmatising or stereotyping young people in care. Best-practice guidelines have previously sought to overcome divergent views of young people and professionals with respect to relationships and sexuality education (Pound et al. 2017). Similarly, in Wales, an innovative guide to forging positive relationships has been developed by young people for young people (Renold 2016). Extending such work with specific consideration of the needs of 'looked after' young people will provide invaluable insights as to when, how and with whom, sexual health and development information should be proffered.

National and local policy recognition

National and local policy recognition of parents in and leaving care is needed which acknowledges and clarifies the supportive obligations of the state as parent. Clarification is needed regarding the expectations on all agencies with corporate parenting responsibility in responding to incidences of pregnancy and parenthood for young people in and leaving care. Such responsibilities extend beyond Children's Services and, in order to ensure holistic and coordinated support responses, the obligations and involvement of key agencies need to be made explicit. The absence of such recognition, together with examples of young people struggling with inadequate support, was described as 'neglect all over again as a care leaver'.

> 'Young people need to know they won't be penalised for asking for help. There is always the threat of Social Services which other parents wouldn't have. To change that, it has to start at the top.' (Advisory group member)

Such recognition should highlight the potential of care-experienced parents, challenge negative assumptions about parenting capacity, but also recognise individual needs and difference.

> 'Really important not to assume everyone is the same and that care leavers will all struggle and need every type of support when they become parents.' (Advisory group member)

Related to this, further debate is required as to the potential role and responsibility of the state as grandparent. Over the course of the consultations, the notion of state as grandparent generated mixed responses. Some expressed concern that ideas of the state as grandparent had the potential to strengthen the mandate for statutory involvement and intervention, and/or legitimise an extended state role in parents' lives, which may be neither wanted nor needed. Consultations also pointed to the feasibility of extending state obligations and adding additional pressures to a system already described as in crisis (Care Crisis Review 2018). Nevertheless, some understood a grandparenting role as a natural extension of the role of parent and argued that if the role of state as parent was to substitute and/or replicate the support ordinarily provided by birth families, then additional help should be prompted by such a significant life event. Moreover, negative comparisons between the experiences of and support available from corporate and birth parents were frequently cited. For example, it is hard to imagine families routinely referring young people for parenting assessment. It is also improbable that parents would have available or think it important to recall masses of historical information to inform assessments of parenting potential. Grandparents in birth families are unlikely to feel constrained or divided in their ability to support both their child and grandchild. Viewed in this way, there are stark disparities in corporate parenting responses to parents in and leaving care, which prompts urgent questions about the ways parents are seen, treated and supported. Related to this, when non-care-experienced young people were asked to discuss the support that they felt would be available to a young parent, grandparents featured heavily in preparing young people for parenthood, accompanying young parents to health appointments and baby groups, providing advice, encouragement and practical support, facilitating returns to education/training, as well as offering help with finances and housing. Viewed in this way, the absence of in-depth consideration and acknowledgement of responsibilities potentially leaves care-experienced young people at significant disadvantage.

Practice guidance to support young people as parents

Practice guidance is required to support professionals in their work with parents in and leaving care. Practice guidance should provide a framework for good practice and include:

- *Reminders of the potential for parents in and leaving care to be stigmatised and face additional adversity and disadvantage.* The importance of non-judgemental approaches, open communication and a commitment to ensuring equality of experience and opportunity should be highlighted. The potential for local authorities to develop or commission training co-produced and/or delivered by care-experienced parents should be explored.
- *Clarification of the circumstances in which agencies should make a referral to Children's Services.* It should be made explicit that referrals based solely on care experience are discriminatory.
- *Clarification of access to and use of historical information to inform parenting assessments.* While recognising the obligations of social workers to consider and monitor risk, there is also a need to recognise the potential for discrimination and disadvantage based on outdated and potentially inaccurate information.

> 'People always trust words on paper rather than the person in front of them. How can you read all the information on a person's file and not judge? Social workers would have to judge the person in front of them if they hadn't been in care and it should be the same for everyone.' (Advisory group member)

- *Advice to professionals in managing dual roles and responsibilities with regard to supporting young people, as well as fulfilling safeguarding responsibilities.* While acknowledging safeguarding responsibilities, young people should not feel that they will be penalised for approaching corporate parents for help.

- *Directions to holistically consider potential support needs.* This includes factors directly and indirectly related to parenting and encompassing practical, emotional and financial considerations. This will likely include needs associated with caring for a baby, as well as housing, health, finances, education, training and employment. For young people whose children will be living with the other biological parent, considerations of emotional and practical support still apply and there may also be a need to consider parental responsibility and visiting opportunities. Austin (2018) has previously stressed the importance of reviewing young people's Pathway Plans when they become parents. In the consultations, young parents advocated the emphasis being on supporting parents to make decisions for themselves, and the potential for young people to co-produce a checklist to support holistic consideration of needs was advocated.

  'The focus needs to be on empowering young people, helping them to help their children.' (Advisory group member)

- *Options for support responses.* While parity of support provision was highlighted in consultations, so too was the need to tailor support to individual needs and circumstances. Some parents will require minimal support while others will require intensive and open-ended support. Options should include both generic family support initiatives as well as provision which takes account of and responds to individual care experience. Expectations for engaging in support should be supported by a clear rationale which can be discussed and explained to parents. The availability of one-to-one support and the option to link parents to peer support initiatives were the most popular during consultations. Developments in the provision of advice and options with respect to support have recently been promoted by Become and Family Rights Group (2020). Similarly, an innovative intensive intervention, adopting a trauma-informed approach, has shown promise in reducing risk, supporting positive change and allowing opportunity for parents to process past experiences (Walsh et al 2019). Such innovation may provide a helpful starting point for ongoing development for families at high risk of separation. Likewise, the importance of working with care-experienced parents to shape and develop local support initiatives was emphasised in order to ensure support that is both acceptable and meaningful. Consultations with care-experienced parents also emphasised that, in the event of psychological or therapeutic support being highlighted as a need, the local authority should commit to ensuring this is provided even in circumstances where children are separated from parents.

- *The development of information for parents by parents.* Work should be undertaken with care-experienced young people to co-produce materials regarding rights and entitlements, and advice and tips, as well as local support options (materials developed by Family Rights Group 2016b and Just for Law Kids 2017a will also be helpful in this regard). Such materials should be available to professionals to distribute to young people to support discussion of needs and support options.

- *Directions to ensure information and access to independent advocacy support at the earliest opportunity.* In the consultations, parents were passionate about the importance of advocacy support. This was seen as ensuring accurate information about rights and entitlements, and strengthening the likelihood that parents would be listened to and treated fairly. Professionals should be able to direct parents to online materials and advice (such as information aimed at young parents produced by Family Rights Group 2016a and Just for Law Kids 2017b) as well as refer young people to locally available in-person support. The availability of advocacy support was not viewed as instead of, or necessarily in conflict with relationships with other professionals. However, the independent position of advocacy workers was highly valued by parents.

> 'Young people may be more likely to engage with someone independent. Bad experiences with Social Services can make people less likely to trust them.' (Advisory group member)

Advocacy was also viewed as a means of strengthening the position of parents. Related to this, consultations with parents also suggested that the option of audio-recording meetings should be available. This proposal was sometimes indicative of previously strained relationships with Children's Services and again provided a means of strengthening parents' position, enabling them to prove what had been said or promised. However, the proposal was also framed more positively, as providing an opportunity for parents to listen back to discussions when they were less emotional or overwhelmed, ensuring that they were clear about concerns and expectations.

These recommendations necessitate commitment and action at national, local and individual levels. It is hoped that the findings and discussion in this book will encourage individual practitioners to show belief in young people's potential, to advocate for equality, and to challenge stigma and discrimination where it is apparent. Such commitment, combined with efforts to work with care-experienced parents and harness their knowledge, insights and expertise, has the potential to make a real difference to young people's experiences. Yet, in order to bring about meaningful and sustained change, it is imperative that senior managers and policy officials also share such commitment, providing the much-needed frameworks and funding to facilitate good practice and help prevent systemic corporate parent/grandparent neglect.

Conclusion

To conclude, the following letter has been written by a member of the parents advisory group. Jen's story both inspired and helped to shape the focus of the Voices research, and the study has benefited from her advice and guidance from the outset. The letter is intended to give the last word of this book to care-experienced parents, and to offer a final heartfelt reminder of the need to recognise and respond to the issue of early pregnancy and parenthood for young people in and leaving care.

> 'My name is Jen, I am in my early thirties and I live with my husband and young son. I am also pregnant and due to give birth to any day. This will be my fifth child but it will be the first time that I go into labour not worrying about Children's Services, not waiting for the conversation with the midwife about the need to inform social workers and not waiting anxiously for their arrival.
>
> 'There are lots of things that will be different this time. I've been able to buy things like a Moses basket, pram, clothes and know they are going to get used. The nursery my husband and I have decorated will welcome my baby from hospital, and this time there will be banners and balloons when I come home. This time I'm looking forward to lots of firsts: first bath time, first smile, first sleep through the night, first words, first birthday, first holiday, first Christmas, first steps. I'm looking forward to these firsts

because they will be with me and the joy they will bring won't be spoilt by a looming visit, meeting or decision.

'It's taken a long time to get to where I am now. My journey with Social Services began at age 3. I have never looked at my file because I haven't wanted to read what was written about me. From what I can remember and what I have been told in the years since, I don't blame social workers for taking me away. However, the 'care' I received from my corporate parents in the years following was also not as good as it should have been.

'I was 17 when I gave birth to my first child. I had been in a relationship with a man who was seven years older than me. It started when I was 13. I had no one warning me about the relationship, trying to tell me it was unhealthy, let alone illegal. I didn't know what sexual exploitation was, or domestic abuse. I had no one talking to me about respecting my body or safe sex. I thought it was love, I thought he was my future and I thought every time he hit me it was because I deserved it. The pregnancy went unnoticed at first but even when my secret was out, there was no proper planning or preparation. Everyone just kept arguing over what should happen to me. At eight months pregnant I was told I had to leave my residential home as that was the only way social workers would do something for me.

'After giving birth I was left in hospital for two weeks because no one knew what to do with me. When it went to court, I was sent to a mother and baby unit for assessment. I passed the assessment, everything was going well apart from housing. They told me I couldn't stay in the unit because of cost and I found myself in the same position again, with nowhere to go, nobody to take me in. My first child ended up in foster care because I agreed to put her needs first; there was a foster place available for her, but not for us both.

'That is how this started, not because of abuse or injury, but because I had nowhere to go and no one to help me.

'There was also no one to offer help or support after I lost my child. My problems got worse and more unhealthy relationships followed. Social workers saw me as a failed mother and my second, third and fourth children were all removed at birth. After giving birth to my third child, I hadn't even delivered the placenta when I was told social workers had been notified. I hadn't made it off the delivery table before I was reminded I wasn't good enough as a mother.

'My two eldest children were adopted and all I can hope is that one day they come to look for me and they understand that I loved and wanted them, but was powerless to stop what happened. My third child is in foster care and I visit as much as I am allowed. With the support of my husband, my fourth child was returned to my care. Having been removed at birth, I was told I would be unlikely to have him back, that I wouldn't be able to parent him, that they were looking at adoption. Within the year, I was being congratulated in court, praised for everything I had done. Social workers are no longer involved with my son and there is no one involved for my unborn baby. Even though I am now seen as a 'good enough' parent, I have been advised that my daughter's needs will be best met with her current carer.

'Some of the things that have happened I wouldn't wish on my worst enemy. There have been times where I've had mental health problems, times where I have turned to alcohol, times when I've sought comfort in abusive relationships, times where I didn't want to be here any more. I haven't always known what is expected of me and some of the things that have been said have been cruel.

'I have been told I am not working with social workers, not 'engaging' as I should. I have also been told I don't need to let them know about every little thing. I've been told I was too emotional: because I cried in court when they said my daughter was going to be adopted, because I cried in the final contact when I knew I wasn't going to see her again, because I cried at missing her first Christmas, because I cried as the foster carer was taking her away. When my child was removed, I was told I was too angry. 'I've been told I wasn't fit to look after a child, told I would never be a parent.

'Thankfully, things are very different for me today. I'm really proud of my life now and I feel grateful because I know a lot of people don't get to this point. I get so much joy from being a parent, from the simplest of things, some of which most people hate – the school runs in the rain, waking in the night, the tantrums, endless "Can I have" or "Why … why … why …".

'But I'm also still affected by what has happened. I am a mother of four, soon to be five, but three of my children are not with me. It's left me with anxiety – if there's a car outside – my first thought is that it's a social worker coming to do a check. I worry that someone has made a new referral and the nightmare will start again.

'I can't and don't regret having my children. I just wish things had been different. I wish that I had met people earlier who made me realise I'm not a bad person. I wish I had known where to go for support. I wish I had known my legal rights a bit more. All of the things that I had later in life, the chance, the support, the relationship, the family, I wish I had that earlier.

'I know that is not the same for everyone and this research has included others who have had worse and better experiences than me. There are some dedicated workers and there are some helpful schemes available. But good support is not available to everyone. It shouldn't be that you are lucky if you have people you can rely on, lucky if you get a good social worker, lucky if you have a strong personal adviser or leaving-care team, lucky if you get good housing, lucky if you get offered a mother and baby place, lucky if get a good solicitor, lucky if the judge is in a good mood. It shouldn't be down to luck. All young people deserve the opportunity to be a parent and to have a family of their own.

'The social workers, managers and professionals who were involved with me made decisions about me and for me, often without care or consultation. If those people had thought of themselves more as parents and grandparents and less as professionals, maybe things would have been different.

'I hope through sharing my experience and being involved in this research, I can help bring about a different experience for others. I hope that the book brings together care-experienced young people and parents, midwives, health visitors, social workers, personal advisers, senior managers, government officials, charity workers, volunteers … anyone and everyone who can make a difference. I hope this is the start of something better.'

References

Action for Children (2017) *The Next Chapter: Young People and Parenthood*, Watford: Action for Children.

Ahrens, K.R., Spencer, R., Bonnar, M., Coatney, A. and Hall, T. (2016) 'Qualitative evaluation of historical and relational factors influencing pregnancy and sexually transmitted infection risks in foster youth', *Children and Youth Services Review*, 61: 245–52.

Ainsworth, M.D.S., Blehar, M.C., Walters, E. and Wall, S. (1978) *Patterns of Attachment*, Hillsdale, NJ: Erlbaum.

Anthony, R., Meakings, S., Doughty, J., Ottaway, H., Holland, S. and Shelton, K.H. (2016) 'Factors affecting adoption in Wales: predictors of variation in time between entry to care and adoptive placement', *Children and Youth Services Review*, 67: 184–90

Aparicio, E., Pecukonis, E.V. and O'Neale, S. (2015) '"The love that I was missing": exploring the lived experience of motherhood among teen mothers in foster care', *Children and Youth Services Review*, 51: 44–54

Austin, E. (2018) 'Top ten tips for advocates from the MAC project: helping care leavers who are parents get a good Pathway Plan', [online] Available from: https://www.dropbox.com/s/jkitenrb3wa84nt/Top%2010%20Tips%20-%20Pathway%20Planning%20%28draft%201%29.docx.pdf?dl=0 [Accessed 3 January 2019].

Bandura, A. (1977) *Social Learning Theory*, Oxford: Prentice Hall.

Barn, R. and Mantovani, N. (2007) 'Young mothers and the care system: contextualizing risk and vulnerability', *British Journal of Social Work*, 37: 225–43.

Batzer, S., Berg, T., Godinet, M.T. and Stotzer, R.L. (2018) 'Efficacy or chaos? Parent–child interaction therapy in maltreating populations: a review of research', *Trauma, Violence, & Abuse*, 19(1): 3–19.

Become and Family Rights Group (2020) 'Advice for care-experienced young parents and parents to be', [online] Available from: https://twitter.com/Become1992/status/1288421582050918406/photo/1 [Accessed 4 August 2020].

Bernard, C. (2015) 'Black Teenage Mothers' Understandings of the Effects of Maltreatment on their Coping Style and Parenting Practice: A Pilot Study', *Children and Society*, 29(5): 355–65.

Biehal, N. and Wade, J. (1996) 'Looking back, looking forward: care leavers, families and change', *Children and Youth Services Review*, 18(4–5): 425–45.

Biehal, N., Clayden, J., Stein, M. and Wade, J. (1992) *Prepared for Living? A Survey of Young People Leaving the Care of Three Local Authorities*, London: National Children's Bureau.

Bilson, A., Featherstone, B. and Martin, K. (2017) 'How child protection's "investigative turn" impacts on poor and deprived communities', *Family Law*, 47: 316–19.

Blazey, E. and Persson, E. (2010) *What Can Professionals Do to Support Mothers Whose Previous Children have been Removed: An Exploratory Study*, London: Children's Workforce Development Council.

Botchway, S.K., Quigley, M.A. and Gray, R. (2014) 'Pregnancy-associated outcomes in women who spent some of their childhood looked after by local authorities: findings from the UK Millennium Cohort Study', *BMJ Open*, 4(12): e005468.

Bourdieu, P. (1984) *Distinction: A Social Critique of the Judgement of Taste*, Cambridge, MA: Harvard University Press.

Bowlby, J. (1969) *Attachment and Loss*: *Vol. 1 Attachment*, New York: Basic Books.

Broadhurst, K. and Mason, C. (2013) 'Maternal outcasts: raising the profile of women who are vulnerable to successive, compulsory removals of their children – a plea for preventative action', *Journal of Social Welfare and Family Law*, 35(3): 291–304.

Broadhurst, K. and Mason, C. (2017) 'Birth parents and the collateral consequences of court-order child removal: towards a comprehensive framework', *International Journal of Law, Policy and the Family*, 31: 41–59.

Broadhurst, K., Mason, C., Bedston, S., Alrouh, B., Morriss, L., McQuarrie, T., Palmer, M., Shaw, M., Harwin, J. and Kershaw, S. (2017) *Vulnerable Birth Mothers and Recurrent Care Proceedings. Final Main Report*, [online] Available from: http://wp.lancs.ac.uk/recurrent-care/files/2017/10/mrc_final_main_report_v1.0.pdf [Accessed 20 July 2020].

Budd, K.S., Holdsworth, M.J. and HoganBruen, K.D. (2006) 'Antecedents and concomitants of parenting stress in adolescent mothers in foster care', *Child Abuse & Neglect*, 30(5): 557–74.

Bullock, R., Courtney, M.E., Parker, R., Sinclair, I. and Thoburn, J. (2006) 'Can the corporate state parent?', *Children and Youth Services Review*, 28(11): 1344–58.

Burns, C. (2018) 'Labels are for clothes not people', [online] Available from: https://www.celcis.org/knowledge-bank/search-bank/blog/2018/11/labels-are-clothes-not-people/ [Accessed 20 July 2020].

References

Bywaters, P., Scourfield, J., Jones, C., Sparks, T., Elliott, M., Hooper, J., McCartan, C., Shapira, M., Bunting, L. and Daniel, B. (2020) 'Child welfare inequalities in the four nations of the UK', *Journal of Social Work*, 20(2): 193–215.

Cameron, C., Hollingworth, K., Schoon, I., van Santen, E., Schröer, W., Ristikari, T., Heino, T. and Pekkarinen, E. (2018) 'Care leavers in early adulthood: how do they fare in Britain, Finland and Germany?', *Children and Youth Services Review*, 87: 163–72.

Care Crisis Review: Options for Change (2018) London: Family Rights Group.

Cashmore, J. and Paxman, M. (1996) *Wards Leaving Care: A Longitudinal Study*, Sydney: NSW Department of Community Services.

Cashmore, J., Paxman, M. and Townsend, M. (2007) 'The educational outcomes of young people 4–5 years after leaving care: an Australian perspective', *Adoption & Fostering*, 31(1): 50–61.

Centre for Social Justice (2015) *Finding their Feet: Equipping Care Leavers to Reach Their Potential*, [online] Available from: https://www.centreforsocialjustice.org.uk/core/wp-content/uploads/2016/08/Finding.pdf [Accessed 20 July 2020].

Chase, E., Warwick, I., Knight, A. and Aggleton, P. (2009) *Supporting Young Parents: Pregnancy and Parenthood among Young People from Care*, London: Jessica Kingsley.

Children's Commissioner for Wales (2016) *The Right Care: Children's Rights in Residential Care in Wales*, Swansea: Children's Commissioner for Wales.

Connolly, J., Heifetz, M. and Bohr, Y. (2012) 'Pregnancy and motherhood among adolescent girls in child protective services: a meta-synthesis of qualitative research', *Journal of Public Child Welfare*, 6: 614–35.

Constantine, W.L., Jerman, P. and Constantine, N.A. (2009) *Sex Education and Reproductive Health Needs of Foster and Transitioning Youth in Three California Counties*, Oakland, CA: Center for Research on Adolescent Health and Development Public Health Institute.

Cook, S.M. and Cameron, S.T. (2015) 'Social issues of teenage pregnancy', *Obstetrics, Gynaecology & Reproductive Medicine*, 25: 243–8.

Corylon, J. and Maguire, C. (1999) *Pregnancy and Parenthood: The Views and Experiences of Young People in Public Care*, London: National Children's Bureau.

Courtney, M., Dworsky, A., Cusick, G.R., Havlicek, J., Perez, A. and Keller, T. (2007) *Midwest Evaluation of the Adult Functioning of Former Foster Youth: Outcomes at Age 21*, Chicago, IL: Chapin Hall at the University of Chicago.

Courtney, M., Dworsky, A., Lee, J. and Raap, M. (2009) *Midwest Evaluation of the Adult Functioning of Former Foster Youth: Outcomes at Age 23 and 24*, Chicago, IL: Chapin Hall at the University of Chicago.

Courtney, M., Dworsky, A., Brown, A., Cary, C., Love, K. and Vorhies, V. (2011) *Midwest Evaluation of the Adult Functioning of Former Foster Youth: Outcomes at Age 26*, Chicago, IL: Chapin Hall at the University of Chicago.

Courtney, M.E., Dworsky, A., Ruth, G., Keller, T., Havlicek, J. and Bost, N. (2005) *Midwest Evaluation of the Adult Functioning of Former Foster Youth: Outcomes at Age 19*, Chicago, IL: Chapin Hall at the University of Chicago.

Craine, N., Midgley, C., Zou, L., Evans, H., Whitaker, R. and Lyons, M. (2014) 'Elevated teenage conception risk amongst looked after children: a national audit', *Public Health*, 128(7): 668–70.

Cresswell, C. (2019) '(Re)Displaying family: relational agency of care-experienced young people embarking on parenthood', in L. Murray, L. McDonnell, T. Hinton-Smith, N. Ferreira and K. Walsh (eds) *Families in Motion: Ebbing and Flowing through Space and Time*, Bingley: Emerald Publishing, pp 233–48.

Cresswell, J.W. and Plano Clark, V.L. (2011) *Designing and Conducting Mixed Methods Research* (2nd edn), Thousand Oaks, CA: Sage.

Critchley, A. (2019a) 'Jumping through hoops: families' experiences of pre-birth child protection', in L. Murray, L. McDonnell, T. Hinton-Smith, N. Ferreira and K. Walsh (eds) *Families in Motion: Ebbing and Flowing Through Space and Time*, Bingley: Emerald Publishing, pp 135–54.

Critchley, A. (2019b) *Quickening Steps: An ethnography of Pre-birth Child Protection*, PhD thesis, unpublished, University of Edinburgh.

Critchley, A. (2020) '"The lion's den": social workers' understandings of risk to infants', *Child & Family Social Work*, online, https://doi.org/10.1111/cfs.12774.

Dalziel, K. and Segal, L. (2012) 'Home visiting programmes for the prevention of child maltreatment: cost-effectiveness of 33 programmes', *Archives of Disease in Childhood*, 97: 787–98.

Del Valle, J.F., Bravo, A., Alvarez, E. and Fernanz, A. (2008) 'Adult self-sufficiency and social adjustment in care leavers from children's homes: a long-term assessment', *Child & Family Social Work*, 13: 12–22.

Department for Children, Schools and Families and Department of Health (2010) *Teenage Pregnancy Strategy: Beyond 2010*, [online] Available from: https://dera.ioe.ac.uk/11277/1/4287_Teenage%20pregnancy%20strategy_aw8.pdf [Accessed 7 August 2017].

Department for Education (2015) *Promoting the Health and Well-being of Looked-after Children: Statutory Guidance for Local Authorities, Clinical Commissioning Groups and NHS England*, [online] Available from: https://www.gov.uk/government/uploads/system/uploads/attachment_data/file/413368/Promoting_the_health_and_well-being_of_looked-after_children.pdf [Accessed 30 January 2017].

Department for Education (2018a) *Applying corporate parenting principles to looked after children and care leavers: Statutory guidance for local authorities*, London: Department for Education.

Department for Education (2018b) *Statistics: Looked After Children*, [online] Available from: https://www.gov.uk/government/collections/statistics-looked-after-children#history [Accessed 21 August 2019].

Department for Education and Skills and Department of Health (2006) *Teenage Pregnancy Next Steps: Guidance for Local Authorities and Primary Care Trusts on Effective Delivery of Local Strategies*, [online] Available from: http://lx.iriss.org.uk/sites/default/files/resources/Teenage%20pregnancy%20next%20steps.pdf [Accessed 20 March 2020].

Department for Health, Social Services and Public Safety (2012) *Standards: Leaving care services in Northern Ireland*, Belfast: DHSSPS.

Dixon, J., Wade, J., Byford, S., Weatherly, H. and Lee, J. (2006) *Young People Leaving Care: A Study of Outcomes and Costs*, York: Social Work Research and Development Unit.

Dominelli, L. (2009) *Introducing Social Work*, Cambridge: Polity Press.

Dominelli, L., Strega, S., Callahan, M., and Rutman, D. (2005) 'Endangered Children: Experiencing and Surviving the State as Failed Parent and Grandparent', *British Journal of Social Work*, 35(7): 1123–44.

Dworsky, A. (2015) 'Child welfare services involvement among the children of young parents in foster care', *Child Abuse & Neglect*, 45: 68–79

Dworsky, A. and DeCoursey, J. (2009) *Pregnant and Parenting Foster Youth: Their Needs, Their Experiences*, [online] Available from: https://www.chapinhall.org/wp-content/uploads/Pregnant_Foster_Youth_final_081109.pdf [Accessed 20 July 2020].

Dwyer, S.C. and Buckle, J.L. (2009) 'The space between: on being an insider-outsider in qualitative research', *International Journal of Qualitative Methods*, 8(1): 54–63.

Elliott, M. (2020) 'Child welfare inequalities in a time of rising numbers of children entering out of home care', *British Journal of Social Work*, 50(2): 581–97.

Engstrom, S. (2019) 'Interpersonal justice: the importance of relationships for child and family social workers', *Journal of Social Work Practice*, 33(1): 41–53.

Fallon, D. and Broadhurst, K. (2015) *Preventing Unplanned Pregnancy and Improving Preparation for Parenthood for Care-experienced Young People*, London: Coram.

Family Rights Group (2016a) 'Young parents advice', [online] Available from: https://www.frg.org.uk/ypa/ [Accessed 3 January 2019].

Family Rights Group (2016b) *Care Leavers*, [online] Available from: https://www.frg.org.uk/ypa/need-help-or-advice/care-leavers [Accessed 3 January 2019].

Featherstone, B., Morris, K. and White, S. (2014) 'A marriage made in hell: early intervention meets child protection', *British Journal of Social Work*, 44(7): 1735–49.

Featherstone, B., Morris, K., Daniel, B., Bywaters, P., Brady, G., Bunting, L., Mason, W. and Nughmana, M. (2017) 'Poverty, inequality, child abuse and neglect: changing the conversation in child protection?', *Children and Youth Services Review*, 97: 127–33.

Featherstone, B., Gupta, A., Morris, K. and White, S. (2018) *Protecting Children: A Social Model*, Bristol: Policy Press.

Ferguson, H. (2011) *Child Protection Practice*, Houndmills: Palgrave Macmillan.

Ferguson, H. (2016) 'What social workers do in performing child protection work: evidence from research into face-to-face practice', *Child & Family Social Work*, 21: 283–94.

Fidler, L. (2018) *In Limbo: Exploring income and housing barriers for reunifying Tasmanian families*, Social Action and Research Centre, [online] Available from: https://www.anglicare-tas.org.au/research/in-limbo-exploring-income-and-housing-barriers-for-reunifying-tasmanian-families/ [Accessed 25 October 2020].

Finnigan-Carr, N.M., Murray, K.W., O'Connor, J.M., Rushovich, B.R., Dixon, D.A. and Barth, R.P. (2015) 'Preventing Rapid Repeat Pregnancy and Promoting Positive Parenting among Young Mothers in Foster Care', *Social Work in Public Health*, 30(1): 1–17.

Forrester D. (2016) 'What, when, why and how: zombie social work and the need for a new narrative', in E. Solomon (ed) *Rethinking Children's Services: Fit for the Future?*, [online] Available from: https://www.catch-22.org.uk/wp-content/uploads/2016/04/Rethinking-Childrens-Services-FINAL.pdf [Accessed 30 November 2017].

Forrester, D. (2020) 'In defense of radical non-intervention: reconsidering Fox Harding's value positions', *Social Work 2020 under Covid-19 Magazine*, 4th edition, 3 June, [online] Available from: https://sw2020covid19.group.shef.ac.uk/2020/06/03/in-defence-of-radical-non-intervention-reconsidering-fox-hardings-value-positions/ [Accessed 13 June 2020].

Foster Jackson, L.J., Beadnell, B. and Pecora, P.J. (2015) 'Intergenerational pathways leading to foster care placement of foster care alumni's children', *Child & Family Social Work*, 20: 72–82.

Fox Harding, L. (1997) *Perspectives in Child Care Policy* (2nd edn), Essex: Prentice Hall.

Furedi, F. (2010) 'Parenting isn't a bunch of skills that can be taught', *Spiked Online*, [online] Available from: http://www.spiked-online.com/newsite/article/9401#.UkFd-cRwZhE [Accessed 20 March 2020].

Furedi, F. (2012) 'Parental determinism: a most harmful prejudice', *Spiked Online*, [online] Available from: http://www.spiked-online.com/site/article/12465/ [Accessed 20 February 2020].

Gardner, F., Leijten, P., Mann, J., Landau, S., Harris, V., Beecham, J. et al (2017) 'Could scale-up of parenting programmes improve child disruptive behaviour and reduce social inequalities? Using individual participant data meta-analysis to establish for whom programmes are effective and cost effective', *Public Health Research*, 5(10).

Gibson, M. (2019) 'The shame and shaming of parents in the child protection process: findings from a case study of an English child protection service', *Families, Relationships and Societies*, 9(2): 217–33.

Gill, A., Grace, R., Waniganayake, M. and Hadley, F. (2020) 'Practitioner and foster carer perceptions of the support needs of young parents in and exiting out-of-home care: A systematic review', *Children and Youth Services Review*, 108: January 2020.

Goffman, E. (1963) *Stigma: Notes on the management of spoiled identity*, New York: Simon & Schuster.

Gupta, A. and Blumhardt, H. (2016) 'Giving poverty a voice: families' experiences of social work practice in a risk-averse system', *Families, Relationships and Societies*, 5(1): 163–72.

Haight, W., Finet, D., Bamba, S. and Helton, J. (2009) 'The beliefs of resilient African-American adolescent mothers transitioning from foster care to independent living: a case-based analysis', *Children and Youth Services Review*, 31(1): 53–62.

Hallett, S. (2016) '"An uncomfortable comfortableness": care, child protection and child sexual exploitation', *British Journal of Social Work*, 46(7): 2137–52.

Haydon, D. (2003) *Teenage pregnancy and looked after children / care leavers*, London: Barnardo's.

Hazan, C. and Shaver, P.R. (1987) 'Romantic love conceptualised as a romantic process', *Journal of Personality and Social Psychology*, 52: 511–24.

Hinton, T. (2018) *Breaking the Cycle: Supporting Tasmanian parents to prevent recurrent child removals*, Social Action Research Centre, [online] Available from: https://www.anglicare-tas.org.au/research/breaking-the-cycle-supporting-tasmanian-parents-to-prevent-recurrent-child-removals/ [Accessed 25 October 2020].

Hyde, A., Fullerton, D., McKeown, C., Dunne, L., Lohan, M. and Macdonald G. (2015) *Sexual Health and Sexuality Education Needs Assessment of Young People in Care in Ireland (SENYPIC): The Perspectives of Key Service-providers: A Qualitative Analysis*, Report No. 3, Dublin: HSE Crisis Pregnancy Programme and Child & Family Agency (Tusla).

Information Analysis Directorate (2018) *Children's Social Care Statistics for Northern Ireland 2017/18*, [online] Available from: https://www.health-ni.gov.uk/publications/childrens-social-care-statistics-northern-ireland-201718 [Accessed 21 August 2019].

James, S., Montgomery, S.B., Leslie, L.K. and Zhang, J. (2009) 'Sexual risk behaviors among youth in the child welfare system', *Children and Youth Services Review*, 31(9): 990–1000.

Just for Law Kids (2017a) *Animated Film – If I Could Talk to Me*, [online] Available from: https://justforkidslaw.org/news/animated-film-if-i-could-talk-me [Accessed 4 Jul 2020].

Just for Law Kids (2017b) *Young Parents*, [online] Available from: https://justforkidslaw.org/what-we-do/empowering-young-people/youth-advocacy/young-parents [Accessed 3 January 2019].

King, B., Putnam-Hornstein, E., Cederbaum, J.A. and Needell, B. (2014) 'A cross-sectional examination of birth rates among adolescent girls in foster care', *Children and Youth Services Review*, 36: 179–86.

Knight, A., Chase, E. and Aggleton, P. (2006) 'Teenage pregnancy among young people in and leaving care: messages and implications for foster care', *Adoption & Fostering*, 30(1): 58–69.

Lewis-Brooke, S., Bell, L., Herring, R., Lehane, L., O'Farrell-Pearce, S., Quinn, K. and So, T. (2017) 'Mothers apart: an action research project based on partnership between a local authority and a university in London, England', *Revista de Asistentă Socială*, 3: 5–15.

Lichtman, M. (2010) *Qualitative Research in Education: A User's Guide*, Thousand Oaks, CA: Sage.

Lieberman, L.D., Bryant, L.L., Boyce, K. and Beresford, P. (2014) 'Pregnant Teens in Foster Care: Concepts, Issues, and Challenges in Conducting Research on Vulnerable Populations', *Journal of Public Child Welfare*, 8(2): 143–63.

Lima, F., Maclean, M. and O'Donnell, M. (2018) *Exploring Outcomes for Children Who Have Experienced Out of Home*, Perth: Telethon Kids Institute.

Long, S., Evans, R., Fletcher., A., Hewitt, G., Murphy, S., Young, H. and Moore, G. (2017) 'A comparison of substance use, subjective wellbeing and interpersonal relationships among young people in foster care and private households: a cross sectional analysis of the School Health Research Network survey in Wales', *BMJ Open*, 7(2): e014198.

Luke, N. and Sebba, J. (2014) *Effective parent-and-child fostering: An international literature review*, Oxford: Rees Centre.

MacBeth, A., Law, J., McGowan, I., Norrie, J., Thompson, L. and Wilson, P. (2015) 'Mellow parenting: systematic review and meta-analysis of an intervention to promote sensitive parenting', *Development Medicine and Child Neurology*, 57: 1119–28.

Mannay, D., Staples, E., Hallett, S., Roberts, L., Rees, A., Evans, R. and Andrews, D. (2015) *Understanding the Educational Experiences and Opinions, Attainment, Achievement and Aspirations of Looked After Children in Wales*, Cardiff: Welsh Government.

Mannay, D., Evans R., Staples, E., Hallett, S., Roberts, L., Rees, A. and Andrews, D. (2017) 'The consequences of being labelled 'looked-after': exploring the educational experiences of looked-after children and young people in Wales', *British Educational Research Journal*, 43(4): 683–99.

Mannay, D., Creaghan, J., Gallagher, D., Mason, S., Morgan, M. and Grant, A. (2018) '"Watching what I'm doing, watching how I'm doing it": exploring the everyday experiences of surveillance and silenced voices among marginalised mothers in Welsh low-income locales', in T. Taylor and K. Bloch (eds) *Marginalized Mothers, Mothering from the Margins*, Advances in Gender Research 25, Bingley: Emerald, pp 25–40.

Mannay, D., Rees, A. and Roberts, L. (2019) 'Introduction', in D. Mannay, A. Rees and Roberts, L. (eds) *Children and young people 'looked after'? Education, intervention and the everyday culture of care in Wales,* Cardiff: University of Wales Press, pp 1–12.

Mantovani, N. and Thomas, H. (2014) 'Choosing motherhood: the complexities of pregnancy decision-making among young black women "looked after" by the state', *Midwifery*, 30: 72–8.

Maxwell, A., Proctor, J. and Hammond, L. (2011) '"Me and my child": parenting experiences of young mothers leaving care', *Adoption & Fostering*, 35(4): 29–40.

McCracken, K., Priest, S., FitzSimons, A., Bracewell, K., Torchia, K. and Parry, W. (2017) *Evaluation of Pause*, [online] Available from: https://www.gov.uk/government/uploads/system/uploads/attachment_data/file/625374/Evaluation_of_Pause.pdf [Accessed 13 March 2018].

Memarnia, N., Nolte, L., Norris, C. and Harborne, A. (2015) '"It felt like it was night all the time": listening to the experiences of birth mothers whose children have been taken into care or adopted', *Adoption & Fostering*, 39(4): 303–17.

Mendes, P. (2009) 'Improving outcomes for teenage pregnancy and early parenthood for young people in out-of-home care: a review of the literature', *Youth Studies Australia*, 28(4): 11–18.

Mendes, P., Pinkerton, J. and Munro, E. (2014) 'Young people transitioning from out-of-home care: an issue of social justice', *Australian Social Work*, 67(1): 1–4.

Morris, K., Mason, W., Bunting, L., Hooper, J., Mirza, N., Brady, G., Bunting, L., Hooper, J., Nughmana, M., Scourfield, J. and Webb, C. (2018) 'Social work, poverty, and child welfare interventions', *Child & Family Social Work*, 1–9, [online] Available from: https://onlinelibrary.wiley.com/doi/abs/10.1111/cfs.12423 [Accessed 17 January 2018].

Morriss, L. (2018) 'Haunted futures: The stigma of being a mother living apart from her child(ren) as a result of state-ordered court removal', *The Sociological Review*, 66(4): 816–31.

Mullins Geiger, J. and Schelbe, L.A. (2014) 'Stopping the Cycle of Child Abuse and Neglect: A Call to Action to Focus on Pregnant and Parenting Youth in and Aging Out of the Foster Care System', *Journal of Public Child Welfare*, 8(1): 25–50.

Murray, S. and Goddard, J. (2014) 'Life after growing up in care: informing policy and practice through research', *Australian Social Work*, 67(1): 102–17.

Muzik, M., Ads, M., Bonham, C., Rosenblum, K.L., Broderick, A. and Kirk, R. (2013) 'Perspectives on trauma-informed care from mothers with a history of childhood maltreatment: A qualitative study', *Child Abuse & Neglect*, 37(12): 1215–24.

National Youth Advocacy Service (NYAS) (2019) 'NYAS Cymru successful charity grant applications!', [online] Available from: https://www.nyas.net/nyas-cymru-successful-charity-grant-applications/ [Accessed 24 July 2020].

Neil, E. (2006) 'Coming to terms with the loss of a child: the feelings of birth parents and grandparents about adoption and post-adoption contact', *Adoption Quarterly*, 10(1): 1–23.

Office for National Statistics (2017) 'Live birth rates to women aged under 18 years and under 20 years, in EU28 countries, 2007, 2016 and 2017', [online] Available from: https://www.ons.gov.uk/peoplepopulationandcommunity/birthsdeathsandmarriages/livebirths/adhocs/009992livebirthratestowomenagedunder18yearsandunder20yearsineu28countries20072016and2017 [Accessed 20 March 2020].

Office for National Statistics (2019) 'Conceptions in England and Wales: 2017', [online] Available from: https://www.ons.gov.uk/peoplepopulationandcommunity/birthsdeathsandmarriages/conceptionandfertilityrates/bulletins/conceptionstatistics/2017 [Accessed 20 March 2020].

Oshima, K.M., Narendorf, S.C. and McMillen, J.C. (2013) 'Pregnancy risk among older youth transitioning out of foster care', *Children and Youth Services Review*, 35(10): 1760–5.

Palmer, C. (2019) 'Positionality and reflexivity: conducting qualitative interviews with parents who adopt children from foster care', in D. Mannay, A. Rees and L. Roberts (eds) *Children and Young People 'Looked After'? Education, Intervention and the Everyday Culture of Care in Wales*, Cardiff: University of Wales Press, pp 155–68.

Pithouse, A. (1987) *Social Work: The Organisation of an Invisible Trade*, Aldershot: Avebury.

Pound, P., Denford, S., Shucksmith, J., Tanton, C., Johnson, A., Owen, J., Hutten, R., Mohan, L., Bonell, C., Abraham, C. and Campbell, R. (2017) 'What is best practice in sex and relationship education? A synthesis of evidence, including stakeholders' views', *BMJ Open*, 7: e014791.

Preston-Shoot, M. (2007) 'Whose lives and whose learning? Whose narratives and whose writing? Taking the next research and literature steps with experts by experience', *Evidence & Policy: A Journal of Research, Debate and Practice*, 3(3): 343–59.

Pryce, J.M. and Samuels, G.M. (2010) 'Renewal and risk: the dual experience of young motherhood and aging out of the child welfare system', *Journal of Adolescent Research*, 25(2): 205–30.

Public Health Wales (2016) *Reducing Teenage Conception Rates in Wales: Project Report*, [online] Available from: http://www.wales.nhs.uk/sitesplus/documents/888/Teenage%20conceptions%20in%20Wales%20%20FINALv1.pdf [Accessed 20 March 2020].

Quinton, D. and Rutter, M. (1984) 'Parents with children in care – I. Current circumstances and parenting', *Journal of Child Psychology and Psychiatry*, 25: 211–29.

Reeves, J. (2006) 'Recklessness, rescue and responsibility: young men tell their stories of the transition to fatherhood', *Practice*, 18(2): 79–90.

Renold, E. (2016) *A Young People's Guide to Making Positive Relationships Matter*, Cardiff University, Children's Commissioner for Wales, NSPCC Cymru/Wales, Welsh Government and Welsh Women's Aid, [online] Available from: http://agendaonline.co.uk/welcome/ [Accessed 2 November 2020].

Roberts, L. (2017) 'A small-scale qualitative scoping study into the experiences of looked after children and care leavers who are parents in Wales', *Child & Family Social Work*, 22: 1274–82.

Roberts, L. (2019) '"A family of my own": when young people in and leaving state care become parents in Wales', in D. Mannay, A. Rees and L. Roberts (eds) *Children and Young People 'Looked After'? Education, Intervention and the Everyday Culture of Care in Wales*, Cardiff: University of Wales Press, pp 140–52.

Roberts, L., Meakings, S., Smith, A., Forrester, D. and Shelton, K. (2017) 'Care leavers and their children placed for adoption', *Children and Youth Services Review*, 79: 355–61.

Roberts, L., Long, S., Young, H., Hewitt, G., Murphy, S. and Moore, G. (2018) 'Sexual health development for young people in state care: cross-sectional analysis of a national survey and views of social care professionals in Wales', *Children and Youth Services Review*, 89: 281–8.

Roberts, L., Maxwell, N. and Elliott, M. (2019) 'When young people in and leaving state care become parents: What happens and why?', *Children and Youth Services Review*, 104(September).

Roca, J.S., García, M.J., Biarnés, A.V. and Rodríguez, M. (2009) 'Analysis of factors involved in the social inclusion process of young people fostered in residential care institutions', *Children and Youth Services Review*, 31(12): 1251–7.

Rolfe, A. (2008) '"You've got to grow up when you've got a kid": marginalized young women's accounts of motherhood', *Community and Applied Social Psychology*, 18(4): 299–314.

Rothenberg, A. (2005) 'Bryan's First 2 Years: Mom, a Group Foster Care Home, and an IFSP', *Zero to Three*, 25(4): 22–9.

Royal College of Nursing (2015) *RCN Survey of Nurses Working with Looked After Children*, [online] Available from: https://www2.rcn.org.uk/__data/assets/pdf_file/0010/608932/004-735.pdf [Accessed 26 January 2017].

Rubin, H.J. and Rubin, I.S. (2012) *Qualitative Interviewing: The Art of Hearing Data* (3rd edn), Thousand Oaks, CA: Sage.

Rutman, D., Strega, S., Callahan, M. and Dominelli, L. (2002) '"Undeserving" mothers? Practitioners' experiences working with young mothers in/from care', *Child & Family Social Work*, 7: 149–59.

Sanders, M., Kirby, J., Tellegen, C. and Day, J. (2014) 'The triple P-Positive Parenting Program: a systematic review and meta-analysis of a multi-level system of parenting support', *Child Psychology Review*, 34: 337–57.

Schwartz, A., Mcroy, R. and Downs, A. (2004) 'Adolescent Mothers in a Transitional Living FacilityAn Exploratory Study of Support Networks and Attachment Patterns', *Journal of Adolescent Research*, 19(1): 85–112.

Scottish Government (2015) *Children and Young People (Scotland) Act 2014, Statutory Guidance on Part 9: Corporate Parenting*, Edinburgh: Scottish Government.

Scottish Government (2018) 'Children's Social Work Statistics 2017/2018', [online] Available from: https://www.gov.scot/publications/childrens-social-work-statistics-2017–2018/ [Accessed 21 August 2019].

Slade, J. (2012) *Safer Caring: A New Approach*, London: The Fostering Network.

Social Care Institute for Excellence (2004) *Preventing Teenage Pregnancy in Looked After Children*, [online] Available from: http://www.scie.org.uk/publications/briefings/briefing09/ [Accessed 20 March 2020].

Social Exclusion Unit (1999) *Teenage Pregnancy*, London: HMSO.

Staples, E., Roberts, L., Lyttleton-Smith, J., Hallet, S. and Voices from Care Cymru (2019) 'Enabling care-experienced young people's participation in research: CASCADE voices', in D. Mannay, A. Rees and L. Roberts (eds) *Children and Young People 'Looked After'? Education, Intervention and the Everyday Culture of Care in Wales*, Cardiff: University of Wales Press, pp 196–209.

StatsWales (2018) 'Children looked after', [online] Available from: https://statswales.gov.wales/Catalogue/Health-and-Social-Care/Social-Services/Childrens-Services/Children-Looked-After [Accessed 21 August 2019].

Stein, M. (2005) *Resilience and Young People Leaving Care: Overcoming the Odds*, York: Joseph Rowntree Foundation.

Stein, M. (2012) *Young People Leaving Care: Supporting Pathways to Adulthood*, London: Jessica Kingsley.

Stockman, K.D. and Budd, K.S. (1997) 'Directions for Intervention with Adolescent Mothers in Substitute Care', *Families in Society*, 78(6): 617–23.

Svoboda, D.V., Shaw, T.V., Barth, R.P. and Bright, C.L. (2012) 'Pregnancy and parenting among youth in foster care: a review', *Children and Youth Services Review*, 34: 867–75.

Swann, C., Bowe, K., McCormick, G. and Kosmin, M. (2003) *Teenage Pregnancy and Parenthood: A Review of Reviews*, London: Health Development Agency.

Taylor, C. and White, S. (2001) 'Knowledge, truth and reflexivity: the problem of judgement in social work', *Journal of Social Work*, 1(1): 37–59.

The Fostering Network (2016) 'Cuts: the view from foster carers. The impact of austerity measures on fostered children and the families that care for them', [online] Available from: https://www.thefosteringnetwork.org.uk/sites/www.fostering.net/files/content/cuts_report.pdf [Accessed 14 June 2020].

Thomas, C. (2018) *The Care Crisis Review: Factors Contributing to National Increases in Numbers of Looked After Children and Applications for Care Orders*, London: Family Rights Group.

Turpel-Lafond, M.E. and Kendall, P. (2009) *Kids, Crime and Care – Health and Well-being of Children in Care: Youth Justice Experiences and Outcomes*, British Columbia, Canada: Office of the Provincial Health Officer.

Tyrer, P., Chase, E., Warwick, I. and Aggelton, P. (2005) '"Dealing with it": experiences of young fathers in and leaving care', *British Journal of Social Work*, 35(7): 1107–21.

Vinnerljung, B. and Sallnäs, M. (2008) 'Into adulthood: a follow-up study of 718 young people who were placed in out-of-home care during their teens', *Child & Family Social Work*, 13: 144–55.

Wade, J. (2008) 'The ties that bind: support from birth families and substitute families for young people leaving care', *British Journal of Social Work*, 38(1): 39–54.

Wakeman, S.E. (2019) 'The language of stigma and addiction', in J.D. Avery and J.J. Avery (eds) *The Stigma of Addiction: An Essential Guide*, New York: Springer, pp 70–80.

Wall-Wieler, E., Almquist, Y., Liu, C., Vinnerljung, B. and Hjern, A. (2018) 'Intergenerational transmission of out-of-home care in Sweden: a population-based cohort study', *Child Abuse & Neglect*, 82: 42–51.

References

Walsh, J., Rudman, H. and Burton, R. (2019) *Evaluation: New Beginnings Greater Manchester Pilot Project*, [online] Available from: https://www.newbeginningsgm.com/evlaution-report-2019 [Accessed 17 July 2020].

Welsh Government (2010) *Sexual Health and Wellbeing Action Plan for Wales 2010–2015*, Cardiff: Welsh Government.

Welsh Government (2012) *Tackling Poverty Action Plan 2012–2016*, [online] Available from: http://www.senedd.assembly.wales/documents/s500001880/CELG4-20-14%20Paper%205.pdf [Accessed 20 March 2020].

Welsh Government (2017) *Families First Programme Guidance*, [online] Available from: https://gov.wales/sites/default/files/publications/2019-07/families-first-guidance-for-local-authorities_0.pdf [Accessed 17 July 2020].

Welsh Government (2018a) *Children Looked After by Local Authorities*, [online] Available from: https://gov.wales/statistics-and-research/children-looked-after-local-authorities/?lang=en [Accessed 22 December 2018].

Welsh Government (2018b) 'Children's Minister announces £15 million to expand services to support families and help reduce the need for children to enter care', [online] Available from: https://gov.wales/childrens-minister-announces-ps15-million-expand-services-support-families-and-help-reduce-need [Accessed 24 July 2020].

Welsh Government (2018c) *Social Services and Well-being (Wales) Act 2014: Part 6 Code of Practice (Looked after and Accommodated Children)*, [online] Available from: https://gweddill.gov.wales/docs/dhss/publications/180328pt6en.pdf [Accessed 26 May 2019].

Welsh Government (2018d) *Wales Children Receiving Care and Support Census*, [online] Available from: https://gov.wales/statistics-and-research/wales-children-receiving-care-support-census/?skip=1&lang=en [Accessed 22 December 2018].

Weston, J.L. (2013) *Care Leavers' Experiences of Being and Becoming Parents*, PhD thesis, unpublished, University of Herefordshire.

Wilkins, D. and Whittaker, C. (2018) 'Doing child-protection social work with parents: what are the barriers in practice?', *British Journal of Social Work*, 48(7), 2003–19.

Winter, V. R., Brandon-Friedman, R.A. and Ely, G.E. (2016) 'Sexual health behaviors and outcomes among current and former foster youth: a review of the literature', *Children and Youth Services Review*, 64: 1–14.

Wolf, D.L. (1996) 'Situating feminist dilemmas in fieldwork', in D.L. Wolf (ed) *Feminist Dilemmas in Fieldwork*, Boulder, CO: Westview Press, pp 1–55.

Index

A

abuse 23, 46, 57, 63, 127
access to support *see* support
accommodation *see* housing
adoption 12, 43, 45, 51, 125, 131
  See also Wales Adoption Study
adversity 23, 24, 50–2, 74, 105, 121, 136
advocacy support 110, 138
agency 75, 95
age of consent 34–5, 133
alcohol 18, 46, 49, 50, 52, 100, 102
anger and resentment 117
antenatal health 1
Anthony, R 44
anxiety and stress 3, 13, 80, 81, 83, 101, 142
Aparicio, E 73, 121
aspirations 36, 73, 78
assessments 12, 29, 60, 67, 118
Attachment Theory 58, 83, 96
austerity 12, 33–4
  See also funding cuts
Austin, E 137
Australia 15, 42
authoritarian 91
availability of support *see* support

B

baby-related equipment 1, 3
balancing responsibilities *see* dual responsibilities
Barn, R 56
Become and Family Rights Group 137
behaviour change 103–5
belonging 73
bereavement 37
best interests of the child 56
Biehal, N 16, 60, 73, 109, 121
birth, placed in care at 44
birth families 108
blame and scrutiny 60
Blazey, E 56
Blumhardt, H 84
bonding 102
book, aims/overview 7–8, 11–14
Botchway, S.K 43
Buckle, J.L 2, 4
Budd, K.S 96
budgeting 49, 52
Bullock, R 10, 128

C

Cameron, C 17
Canada 15
Cardiff University 2, 5
care-experienced parents, perspectives of 73–80, 80–7
care proceedings 43
care system 29–37
caring for a child 101, 137
Centre for Social Justice 43
challenges 52, 73, 85, 86, 91, 92, 96, 100, 120
Chase, Elaine 43, 56
Child Assessment Report for Adoption (CARA) 11, 44
child benefits 4
childhood abuse 24, 46, 51
childhood adversity 46
child protection 42, 49, 63, 65, 68, 84, 110, 124
children's nurse 29, 31, 34
children's rights 9
Children's Social Care Research and Development Centre (CASCADE) 2, 5–7
child sexual exploitation 36
child welfare inequalities 8
choices *see individual choices*
collective responsibility 33
common needs 97
communication 65, 90, 136
condoms 23, 24, 38
confidence 79
conflicted responsibilities 56
Connolly, J 71, 92
consent 19, 23, 24, 34–5, 38
consistency of support *see* support
contraception 19, 23, 30, 31, 36, 39, 75, 76, 133
  pill, the 24, 25, 38
controlling behaviour 101
Cook, S.M 17
corporate parenting 10, 13, 84, 92, 126, 128, 134
  failures 41–4, 50–2, 114, 121
  responsibility 19, 34–5, 55
  and systemic disadvantage 70–1
Corylon, J 73
Courtney, M 43
Craine, N 25
Cresswell, C 5, 74

159

criminal behaviour 46, 111
Critchley, A 65, 82
cross-sectional design 131
cycle of deprivation 43

D

deCoursey, J 16
depression 43
determination, parental 103–6, 121
development concerns 46
digital media 38
disadvantage 8, 13, 17, 52, 64–71, 129, 131, 136
discrimination 8, 12, 56, 58, 60, 62, 63, 118, 127, 131
diversity 132
divided loyalties 67, 71, 112
Dixon, J 16, 56
dolls 32, 34
domestic violence 46, 52, 101–2
Dominelli, L 106
drugs 101, 102, 111, 117
dual responsibilities 55–6, 64–70, 84, 112, 124, 126, 127, 136
Dworsky, A 16
Dwyer, S.C 2, 4

E

early parenthood 15
early pregnancy 6, 12, 15–18, 38–40, 73, 123–4, 133–4
early sexual behaviours 25
education, training or employment 36, 42, 43, 46, 47, 49, 98, 137
effective practice *see* professional practice
emergency contraception 25
emotional abuse 46
emotional bonds 77, 86
emotional health 18
emotional support *see* support
emotional trauma 92
empowerment 137
engaging with professionals 104–6, 120, 121
England 129
England and Wales 16, 38, 41
equality 59–64, 139
ethics 5, 39
ethnographic study 65
evidence 6, 8, 15, 38, 42, 50, 61, 97, 124
exclusion 74
expectations of practice *see* professional practice
experiences of support *see* support

F

failure as a parent 90, 92
family and the state 9, 37
family planning 133
Family Rights Group 137
fathers 16, 23, 24, 25, 41–5, 49, 50, 51, 74, 130
Featherstone, B 114, 121
females 47, 48, 49, 98
Ferguson, H 60, 65
financial support *see* support
Finland 15
Finnigan-Carr, N.M 97
fluctuating demand 113, 122
formal support *see* support
Forrester, D 10, 129
foster care 18, 23, 42, 48, 96, 106, 107, 110, 120, 140
Fox Harding, Lorraine 9, 126–8
free university education 4
friends and family 42, 48, 50, 107, 121
funding cuts 12, 33–4, 39, 124

G

Germany 15
Gibson, M 85
Gill, A 96
girls 36, 37, 66
Goddard, J 96
'good enough' parenting 10
good parenting 58
grandparents 19, 97, 107, 114, 121, 124, 129, 135, 142
Great Britain 15
grief and loss 8, 37, 51, 89
group sessions 112
growing up 73
guidance 124
Gupta, A 84

H

Haight, W 74
Hallett, S 36
hardship 8, 73
Haydon, D 55, 73, 95
health 18, 47, 52, 124
Health and Care Research Wales 5
Health and Wellbeing Survey 18–28
health visitors 109, 110
healthy eating 18
high-income 43
histories, personal 51, 56, 66–7, 70, 82, 91, 124, 136
holistic approach 137
home visits 65, 96
hostels 101, 111

housing 9, 47, 49, 52, 90, 97, 100, 108, 111, 122, 126, 137

I

Illinois 15, 42, 96
images, sexually explicit 24, 38
impersonal identity 128
implants, contraceptive 34
income support 4
Incredible Years 96
independent living 49, 52, 99, 124
individual behaviours/choices 33, 35–7, 104, 121, 125
inequalities 8, 17, 25, 106
informal support *see* support
information and discussion 32
information materials 138
'in-house parent' 112
injustice 82, 88, 89, 129, 132
interference 55, 74, 92, 96
intergenerational experience 71, 79–80, 91, 104, 124, 129
interventions 12, 50, 65, 95, 126
  risks/threats of 55, 73, 80–1, 91–2, 125
  types of 9–10, 97, 110, 116
interviews with professionals 29
intimacy 57
Iowa 15, 42

J

judgemental 55, 67, 96, 124, 136
justifying decisions 61

K

kinship living arrangements 18, 19, 24
Knight, A 55

L

language 10–11
learning difficulties 46, 50, 52
legal status 9
Lieberman, L.D 97
limited resources 33–4, 39
'live-in' parenting 110
living arrangements 9, 19, 20–2, 26–8, 47, 48
living independently 101
local authorities 6, 16, 19, 29, 34, 42, 46, 47, 50–2, 129
Long Acting Reversible Contraception (LARCs) 23, 25, 39
long-term support 114
love 8, 37, 57, 75, 79, 86, 105
low birth weight 43, 46

M

males 16, 47, 48, 49, 98
Mannay, D 132
Mantovani, N 55, 56
maternity grant 4
Maxwell, A 74
McGuire, C 73
means-tested grant 4
Mellow Parenting 96
Mendes, P 42, 126
mental health 18, 49, 50, 90, 97, 102, 117, 122
mental illness 46
methodology 5, 18, 44
middle-class 'good parenting' 55
Midwest Study 15, 42
midwives 109, 110
milk tokens 4
Millennium Cohort Study 43
missed opportunities 52
mistrust 55
mixed methods 5
monitoring 1, 55, 74, 114, 118, 119, 127, 132–3
moral beliefs 76
moral fidelity 97
Morriss, K 89
mother and baby groups 109, 110, 111, 115, 119
motherhood, positive about 74, 86
mothers 23, 24, 41–6, 51, 74, 86, 95, 101, 111, 130
motivation 73, 87, 96
moving home 95, 112
multiple support needs 97–103
Murray, S 96

N

National Youth Advocacy Service 111
needs, understanding 120
neglect 8, 46, 51
network, support *see* support
non-care leaver parents 11
North American states 15
Northern Ireland 41
nurse 30

O

obligations of the state 134
official recordings/statistics 17, 39, 41, 51, 53, 133
outcomes 12, 41–8, 123–5

P

Palmer, C 3
parental determination 58, 103–6

parental support 136–9
parent and child placements 112
Parent-Child Interaction Theory 96
parenthood 12, 37, 42, 57, 75–80, 85–90, 116, 124, 125, 130
parenting capacity 42, 61, 62, 99, 135
parenting 'success' 9, 10, 41–4, 57–8, 85–7, 125
partners 101–2, 103, 107, 117
paternalism 9
Pathway Plans 30, 137
patriarchy 9
peer support 96, 113
penalisation 117, 136
personal experience of parents 97
Persson, E 56
physical activity 18
physical health 50
pill, the *see* contraception
Pithouse, A 8
planning procedures 56
Plano Clark, V.L 5
policies 56
poorer sexual outcomes 12, 39
poor outcomes 8, 43, 52, 92, 125, 132
positive choices 73, 74, 85
positive responses to support 115–16
poverty 9, 74, 78, 126
practical help/guidance 121, 136–9
practitioner skills 65
pre-birth assessment 59, 61, 63
pre-birth child protection 65, 82
pregnancy and parenthood 7
pregnancy planning 9
'presumed incompetency' 71
procedures and planning 30, 59–64, 84, 91
professionals 7, 25, 91, 104–6, 122, 126–9
  confidence in the system 30–4, 39
  dilemmas/dual responsibilities 12, 13, 35, 64–9
  perspectives of 29–30, 55–8, 130
  policy and practice 41, 43, 59–64, 70–1, 123, 131–9
Project Unity 111
protecting children 10
protectionist stance 127
Pryce, J.M 73
Public Health Wales 39
public scrutiny 60
punitive 8, 92

Q

qualitative interviewing 5
Quinton, D 107

R

race 74
referral and assessment 60, 70, 84, 136
relationship-based working 65
relationships 18, 58, 84–5, 90, 100, 108, 134, 140
  with professionals 65–9, 126–9
  and sex 35–7
  status of 48–9
removals of children 43, 51, 104
repeat pregnancy 16, 92
research 2–4, 5–7, 55, 129
resilience 50–2, 66, 67, 83, 121, 125
resources, reduced 33–4, 39, 96, 126, 128
responses, strengthen 132
responsibility 103, 104, 132
rights and entitlements 9, 138
risk-averse practice 18, 47, 56, 60, 61, 120
risk of intervention/referral 55, 64
risky sexual behaviour 6, 13, 15, 25, 29, 36, 38–40, 52, 129
role confusion 96
role models 57, 73
Rolfe, A 73
Rothenburg, A 107
routine referral 61, 81, 124, 127
Rubin, H.J 5
Rutman, D 55, 56
Rutter, M 107

S

safeguarding 13, 56, 61, 66, 68, 71, 84, 120, 127, 136
safer care systems 57
safe sex 31, 32
safety and wellbeing 13
Samuels, G.M 73
School Health Research Network (SHRN) 6, 17, 18–28, 123, 131
Scotland 41
secondary schools 18
self-esteem 32, 36
senior management 39
separation 12, 42, 50, 52, 55, 73, 80, 88, 91, 125, 127
sexual abuse 46, 102
sexual health advice and support 12, 30, 34, 39, 75, 133
sexual health behaviours/risks 7, 16, 26–8, 35, 134
sexual health outcomes 15, 25, 29, 123
sexually explicit images 19, 24, 38
shame and shaming 85, 89
shared responsibility 33
single fathers 23, 24, 25

single mothers 23, 24
smoking 18
social and economic disadvantage 17, 43
Social Learning Theory 58
socially acceptable role 73, 77
Social Services and Wellbeing (Wales) Act 2014 128
social support 97
social workers 29, 55, 84–5
Spain 15
specialist interventions 95
stability 73
state, the 8, 9, 13, 127, 134
statutory support 47
Stein, M 92
stereotypes 64
stigmatisation 10, 58, 67, 70, 79, 83, 91, 96, 118, 127
Stockman, K.D 96
struggling with parenthood 87–90
substance use 18, 46, 49, 50, 52, 100, 101
supper clubs 110
support 10, 30–3, 47, 55, 68, 87, 91, 124–5, 128
  emotional 13, 56, 86
  experiences of 115–20
  formal/informal 106–9, 109–15, 121, 122
  inadequate 74, 134
  needs 29, 49, 50, 52, 60, 90, 95–103, 137
survey data 7
Svoboda, D.V 92
Sweden 15
systemic disadvantage 70–1
system responses 55

T

teenage mothers 95
teenage pregnancy 12, 16–18, 25, 38
  See also early pregnancy
tensions 13
termination of pregnancy 16, 76
themes 8–10
therapeutic support 138
Thomas, C 55

threats to care system 33–7
timing 34–5
transactional sex 16
transformative experience 92
transport 100
Triple P 96
Tyrer, P 74

U

understanding, shared 126
unemployment 46
unhelpful support 84, 92, 116, 118–19
United Kingdom 42, 43, 129, 130, 133
United States 15, 16, 17, 25, 42
Unity project 116
universal services 109, 113
university education 4
unplanned pregnancy 18, 38–9, 52

V

value perspectives 9, 66, 126–8
violence, exposure to 46, 82, 111
Voices from Care Cymru (VfCC) 15, 17, 29–30, 46, 56–9, 74–8, 122, 130, 132
vulnerability 25, 38–9, 43, 51, 56, 60, 91

W

Wade, J 16, 73, 74, 109, 121
Wakeman, S.E 10
Wales 1, 5, 16, 29, 41, 51, 111, 115, 130, 131
Wales Adoption Study 6–7, 11, 12, 43–50, 125
welfare benefits 4, 46
wellbeing 9, 18
Weston, J.L. 86
Whittaker, C 65
Wilkins, D 65
Wisconsin 15, 42
Wolf, D.L 4
women 16, 43, 74, 103, 107
workloads 124, 128